FROM SKEDADDLE TO SELFIE

From Skedaddle to Selfie

WORDS OF THE GENERATIONS

Allan Metcalf

OXFORD
UNIVERSITY PRESS

OXFORD
UNIVERSITY PRESS

Oxford University Press is a department of the University of
Oxford. It furthers the University's objective of excellence in research,
scholarship, and education by publishing worldwide.

Oxford   New York
Auckland   Cape Town   Dar es Salaam   Hong Kong   Karachi
Kuala Lumpur   Madrid   Melbourne   Mexico City   Nairobi
New Delhi   Shanghai   Taipei   Toronto

With offices in
Argentina   Austria   Brazil   Chile   Czech Republic   France   Greece
Guatemala   Hungary   Italy   Japan   Poland   Portugal   Singapore
South Korea   Switzerland   Thailand   Turkey   Ukraine   Vietnam

Oxford is a registered trademark of Oxford University Press
in the UK and certain other countries.

Published in the United States of America by
Oxford University Press
198 Madison Avenue, New York, NY 10016

Library of Congress Cataloging-in-Publication Data
Metcalf, Allan A., author.
From skedaddle to selfie: words of the generations / Allan Metcalf.
pages cm
Includes index.
ISBN 978–0–19–992712–8 (hardback)—ISBN 978–0–19–992713–5 (ebook)—
ISBN 978–0–19–026346–1 (ebook)   1. English language—United States—New words.
2. English language—United States—Lexicology.   3. English language—Social aspects—
United States.   4. Language and culture—United States.   5. English language—New words.
6. Americanisms.   7. Lexicology.   I. Title.
PE2830.M374 2015
427'.973—dc23
2015023136

1 3 5 7 9 8 6 4 2
Printed in the United States of America
on acid-free paper

CONTENTS

PREFACE

Generating this Book

Generations generate interest these days. The deepest divisions in our society, it is argued, are not matters of gender or race or religion or region, but of membership in different generations, a matter of destiny depending simply on when each of us was born. We are told about the seemingly self-centered Millennials (born 1982–2004) populating our schools and entering the workplace, as they clash with their elders, the hardscrabble Generation Xers (born 1961–1981) and they in turn with their elders, the indulgent Boomers (born 1943–1960, by one reckoning). Not to mention the remnants of the compromising Silent Generation (born 1925–1942) and the heroic G.I. Generation (born 1901–1924). Or for that matter the incoming Homeland Generation (born 2005–), poised to make their linguistic mark soon as teenagers.

Where did this concern for generations come from? For guidance I turned to the book that started it all, *Generations* by William Strauss and Neil Howe, published in 1990, and their sequel, *The Fourth Turning*, published in 1997. There in generous detail they advance the theory that all of American history can be seen as a progression of an eighty-year cycle of clashing generations, each with its distinctive values and attitudes toward people and events. And maybe it can.

But amid their copious examples of the people, declarations, and actions distinguishing one generation from another, one thing is missing: the distinctive words that we would expect to go with the distinctive attitudes. So I started looking for them myself, and the result was this book. It doesn't pretend to be exhaustive, just to present salient examples of the words that go with the generations.

There's no automatic way of determining which words belong to which generation. There's no algorithm that separates out the words of the Millennials (like *selfie*) from those of Generation X (like *grunge* or *whatever*), for example. And most words plausibly associated with a particular generation are known to, and often much used by, other generations. It's a judgment call, so much so that if I were doing this book all over again, some of my choices wouldn't be the same.

But many of them would be. In doing my research, I have found general agreement about the generational attachment of certain words. And I have had much help, both from databases available on the Internet and from individuals belonging to the recent generations.

Dictionaries ranging from the *Oxford English Dictionary* to the *Historical Dictionary of American Slang*, the *Dictionary of American Regional English*, and the user-generated Urbandictionary.com have provided suggestions of words to look for and examples of usage. But in this age of the Infosphere, I have also been fortunate to have vast quantities of texts and blogs and tweets and other posts searchable with the click of a mouse to capture words as they are actually used.

For the earlier generations, the copious contents of Google Books have been invaluable, providing contemporary contexts for earlier words. So have the Corpus of Historical American English and the website Making of America, among others. Google Ngrams is very helpful in charting the popularity of words over the past five hundred years.

For the present day and its mixture of Millennials, Xers, Boomers, and Silents, numerous individuals have provided (sometimes unwittingly) suggestions and examples of how their words and those of neighboring generations are used. There are so many I haven't been able to keep track of them all, but I do want to thank:

Word experts David Barnhart, Gerald Cohen, Joan Hall, Erin McKean, Wendalyn Nichols, Barry Popik, Fred Shapiro, Diana Solomon, Jane Solomon, Sali Tagliamonte, Ben Yagoda, and Ben Zimmer;

Friends, family, and acquaintances Cat Flynn, Khara Koffel, Beverly Johns, David Metcalf, Goran Metcalf, Sara Metcalf, Beth Oberg, Nathan Solow, Steven Wheatley, and Jeannie Zeck. And special appreciation to my wife, Donna Metcalf.

And then, for plentiful help in the various stages of making this book a reality, at Oxford University Press I must thank my editor Peter Ohlin, and Hallie Stebbins, Kendra Millis, Kimberly Craven, and Ryan Cury.

FROM SKEDDADLE TO SELFIE

INTRODUCTION

Speaking of the Generations

At first glance the whole notion seems absurd. William Strauss and Neil Howe would have us believe that all people born in the United States during a particular twenty-year stretch are alike in their attitudes toward life and toward the historical events they encounter. Not only are all members of a generation the same in their attitudes, but the attitudes are different from those of the generation before them and the generation after.

And not only that. In their books *Generations* (1990) and *The Fourth Turning* (1997), Strauss and Howe want us to believe that the generations repeat themselves in eighty-year cycles, approximately the length of a long human life. After four very different generations, they say, a fifth comes along that is like the first, a sixth like the second, and so on. The generations come in four varieties, they say, always in the same sequence: artist (adaptive), prophet (idealistic), nomad (reactive), and the greatest of all, hero (civic).

The artist generation, they explain, grows up in the shadow of the heroes of the preceding generation. Awed by those heroes (for example, the G.I. generation that fought World War II), the artists are sensitive but indecisive (for example, the Silent Generation born 1925–1942). Next come the prophets, "narcissistic young crusaders" both idealistic and obnoxious, most recently represented by the Baby Boomers. After them comes a neglected, alienated nomad generation—our Generation X. And then again come the heroes, facing a crisis and overcoming it. The generation known as Millennials (born 1982–2004, according to Strauss and White's reckoning) belongs to this hero category, they say. Starting around 2005, they predicted a decade earlier, there will come a crisis, and the "mannerly, civic-spirited, and emotionally placid" Millennials will take the lead in overcoming the crisis in the middle 2020s.

This pattern of generations, they say, goes back not just to the past century, but before the founding of the United States. Indeed, in Anglo-American culture they claim it goes back even further, before the very first English-speaking settlements in North America to a "Reformation generation" in England at the end of the 15th century.

Because these generations go in cycles, Strauss and Howe find it possible to forecast the attitudes of generations yet unborn. Accordingly, their 1990 book *Generations* elaborating this theory has the immodest subtitle: *The History of America's Future, 1584 to 2069.*

And they were only getting started. Their 1997 sequel, *The Fourth Turning: An American Prophecy: What the Cycles of History Tell Us about America's Next Rendezvous with Destiny*, connected the turning points in American history to the generations. The "turnings," they said, occur when a new generation begins to be born and the previous generations move from youth (ages 0–21) to rising adulthood (22–43) to midlife (44–65) to elder (66–87). The first turning is a collective high, with everybody happy as a result of overcoming a recent crisis. Then comes an awakening, led by young-adult prophets. Then follows an unraveling, as the nomads disagree with the middle-aged prophets. Finally, every eighty years or so, the turning is a crisis, a point of climax, brought to a successful outcome by the young-adult heroes: the American Revolution, the Civil War, World War II, and then the current crisis, which they confidently say will reach its climax in or about the year 2025.

Whew. Can you believe that?

Don't we know, from our own experience, that other people our age aren't exactly like us? Some are assertive, some are shy, some are lazy, some are industrious, some are careless, some are careful, some are mean, some are generous, and so on. How can we all share the same attitudes, especially when this includes those born before and after us over a twenty-year stretch? It's like we're being asked to believe in astrology. (And of course, many of us do.)

On the other hand, don't we also know that the American character is permanent and unchanging? Read Tocqueville's

Democracy in America, written nearly two centuries ago, and you'll see Americans there pretty much as we see ourselves today: pragmatic, down to earth, resourceful, generous, clubbable.

Undaunted by those extremes of variability and invariability, Strauss and Howe calmly and persistently make their point, adducing page after page of evidence (more than 500 pages of small print in *Generations*, more than 300 pages of slightly larger print in *Fourth Turning*) to show that the members of one generation indeed share attitudes different from those of another.

For example—and Strauss and Howe are generous with examples—there's the generation long known as Baby Boomers. Demographers named it because of the postwar American boom in births lasting from 1946 to 1964. For Strauss and Howe, the birth years of those who have the Boomer attitude are 1943 to 1960. Either way, Boomers encompass the first decade and a half after World War II.

And these Boomers, Strauss and White say, as members of a prophet generation, are idealists. But also, less charitably, they are smug and self-absorbed, the other side of the coin of idealism. Boomers were student rebels in their youth, yuppies in rising adulthood, moralists in midlife. Boomers, the authors say in *Generations*, "have metamorphosed from Beaver Cleaver to hippie to braneater to yuppie to what some are calling 'Neo-Puritan'. . . ." Among the famous Boomers presented as examples are Patty Hearst, Donald Trump, Oprah Winfrey, Bill Gates, and (later) George W. Bush. Remember that recent president? He called himself "the decider," a perfect label for the attitude his generation is said to take.

The authors made some predictions that seem accurate. "Boomers are starting to show a fascination for apocalyptic solutions," wrote Strauss and Howe back in 1990, more than a decade before Boomer George W. Bush led the nation into war against Saddam Hussein's Iraq, even though Iraq had nothing to do with the 9/11 attacks and didn't have the weapons of mass destruction used as justification for the war.

Another decade later, the Tea Party demanding no compromise on the federal debt-limit or raising taxes was led by a Boomer, Judson Phillips, born circa 1959. The Republican speaker of the House of Representatives during that time was John Boehner, another Boomer, born 1949. Speaking calmly and arguing for a compromise was President Obama, born in 1961 just after the Boomer years, member of the quite different Generation X. With copious examples of this sort, the notion of generations begins to persuade.

And it's not as if Strauss and Howe invented the idea of generations, or of the Baby Boom. The increase in births after World War II was hard to ignore. Long before Strauss and Howe, we were taking about and watching Boomers as their numbers grew.

Preceding the Boomers, in Strauss and Howe's analysis, were the Silent Generation. Again it wasn't Strauss and Howe who first used that label; it was applied by their worried elders in the 1950s. So silent were they that, as Strauss and Howe point out, unlike all previous generations none of their members has ever become president of the United States. As the Silents settle into their old age, it seems certain that none of them will.

At any time there are four living generations, interacting with each other, along with a remaining few of an earlier generation and the beginnings of a later one. In the early 21st century there are the Silents (born 1925–1942), Boomers (going by attitude rather than birth records, born 1943–1960), Generation X (1961–1981), and Millennials (1982–2004). The Homeland Generation (2005–) is just getting started. And there are still a few living members of the heroic G.I. Generation, born 1901 through 1924.

But how do these generations display their differences? And how do we learn about each generation's particular preoccupations, pleasures, view of the world, and their place in it?

The answer is, through the words they use. And that's what this book is about—the words that make each generation distinctive.

Take the Boomers, for example. Their name comes from the demographic fact of the postwar increase in births, but it remains well known because *Boomers* so aptly reflects their loud, obtrusive presence in every age of their existence. They were the *hippies* of the 1960s, the first (and surely the last) to call themselves *groovy* in their teen years and early adulthood. They revealed themselves in the fad for *streaking* in the early 1970s. As they matured, they were the first *yuppies*. Later they became *helicopter parents* of Millennials. And Boomer President George W. Bush spoke for his generation when he called himself *the decider*.

Or consider their predecessors, the Silent Generation, born 1925–1942 according to Strauss and Howe's analysis. They were the first to think of themselves, and to be viewed by others, as *teenagers.* Previous generations had indeed also gone from children to adults, but they didn't think of themselves entering a special age when they were 13. In their teen years, the Silents were also the first to be *babysitters* and *bobbysoxers*, and the first to listen to *rock and roll.*

The G.I. Generation, born 1901–1924, were the first to think of themselves, and to be viewed by others, as G.I.s when serving in the military in World War II. They fought and won World War II, but they were also the first to have *boyfriends* and *girlfriends* and to dance the *jitterbug.* In later years, they were the first to be called *senior citizens.*

Going back yet further, the Lost Generation that fought World War I and then fueled the Roaring Twenties was the first to be *sexy.* Or at least the first to use that word. They also were the first to appreciate that new kind of American music known as *jazz.*

Current generations too have their distinctive vocabulary. Generation X, born 1961 through 1981, had its *slackers, hackers, geeks*, and *nerds.* They put *you guys* and *hey* in everyone's vocabulary and responded to the world with *whatever.*

The most recent generation, the Millennials, born in 1982 through 2004, became the first to *friend* and *unfriend* over the Internet, thanks to the invention of Facebook by one of their own, Mark Zuckerberg (born 1984). They invented *hipsters* and *selfies* and took part in *flash mobs.* They were so comfortable with communicating by technology that they were often *awkward* in person. Their FOMO (fear of missing out) led to *yolo* and *LOL*.

Every generation has intimate relations, or there wouldn't be a next generation. But the kinds of relations keep changing. After the *sexy* Lost Generation, the G.I. generation indulged in *necking* and *petting*, Silents were *going steady*, Boomers *hooked up*, and Millennials had *friends with benefits*.

And the Homeland Generation, born 2005 and later? Well, we'll have to *wait* and see.

This book follows Strauss and Howe's well-argued chronology with a chapter for each generation, beginning with the Republican generation that fought the American Revolution. Each chapter presents a few notable words that characterize a generation, in context, with greatest emphasis on the generations still living.

SOME CAVEATS

This is a work of art, not science. It uses Strauss and Howe's scheme as inspiration, not dogma. It uses words I have chosen, not at random nor by some algorithm, but simply because they seem to me to best illuminate the ideas and attitudes of particular eras. Out of hundreds or even thousands of words that could be associated with each particular generation, I have selected a few that seem particularly revealing.

It's highly subjective. If I were doing it over again, I'm sure the list wouldn't be quite the same.

I have, however, tried to stick to the facts. Most of my examples are of words as they were actually used by members of the relevant generations. But my choices of which words to use are anything but objective.

Looking for the first known instance of a word is relatively easy. But that's not what this book is about. For this book, let it be clear, I have looked not for the first use but for the moment when a word reached its apex of use or when it attained its modern meaning, thanks to a particular generation.

And it's not always easy to know which generation to credit for a word. At any given time, at least four generations are alive. Which one owns the word? Which one popularized it? Which one later changed it?

Speakeasy, for example, became widespread only with the advent of Prohibition in the young adulthood of the Lost Generation, but it was known and used earlier. *Trick or treat* was used by a few forerunners of the Silent Generation, but Silent was the generation that put it to wide use. And *dude*—well, that had quite a different meaning for the Progressive Generation in the 19th century than it does today.

You guys, for another example, was in use for many generations before Generation X (in my opinion) made it the normal plural of *you,* and *gay* had quite a different primary meaning until Generation X turned it around. And *occupy* had been around for centuries before the Millennials gave it a twist.

Well, my guess is as good as yours. I hope you'll enjoy these results while you take them with a grain of salt.

THE REPUBLICAN
GENERATION

(born 1742–1766)

The thought heard round the world, the Declaration of Independence of 1776, was the work primarily of a young adult in what Strauss and Howe call the Republican Generation. Its leading and most influential representative was Thomas Jefferson, born 1743, and his, for the most part, are the words of the Declaration.

UNALIENABLE

"We hold these truths to be self-evident, that all men are created equal, that they are endowed by their Creator with certain unalienable Rights, that among these are Life, Liberty and the pursuit of Happiness."

Young Tom Jefferson wasn't the first to use this *unalienable*, but he was responsible for a spike in its popularity, as recorded by Google Ngrams, much greater than ever before or since. From 1776 to the early 1780s, it was his declaration in the Declaration that provoked responses such as John Lind's *Answer to the Declaration of the American Congress* (London, 1776): "If the right of enjoying life be unalienable, whence came their invasion of his Majesty's province of Canada?"

Inalienable, which had been an alternative but less used form of the word in the 18th century, became the dominant form by 1830, shortly after Jefferson's death. Nowadays *unalienable* has a distinctively old-fashioned look, perhaps because it is so indelibly attached to Jefferson and the Declaration.

NATURE'S GOD

"When in the Course of human events, it becomes necessary for one people to dissolve the political bands which have connected them with another, and to assume among the powers of the earth, the separate and equal station to which the Laws of Nature and of Nature's God entitle them, a decent respect to the opinions of mankind requires that they should declare the causes which impel them to the separation."

Nor was Jefferson the first to write of *Nature's God*, the Deist Enlightenment belief that studying nature would lead to the nature of the God that created nature. A poetic elegy for the physicist Robert Boyle, for example, in 1694 declared:

He clearly now does Nature's God adore,
Whom in his Works he darkly saw before.

And Alexander Pope, in his *Essay on Man* (1734), wrote:

Slave to no sect, who takes no private road,
But looks thro' Nature, up to Nature's God:
Pursues that Chain which links th' immense design,
Joins heav'n and earth, and mortal and divine;

Jefferson's contribution was to employ this nicely ambiguous term as the ultimate justification for America's independence. It can be interpreted as strictly Christian, with "Nature's God" simply another name for the God of the Bible who created and rules all Nature. It can be interpreted as nonsectarian, a God who is manifested through the works of Nature and variously understood by different cultures. And it can be interpreted as atheist, reducing God to the laws of Nature as revealed by scientists, not priests.

The phrase thus encompasses a wide range of beliefs about religion, Nature, and God. It encourages tolerance of all beliefs and leads to the First Amendment to the U.S. constitution, the first item in the Bill of Rights, drafted by another member of the Republican Generation, James Madison (born 1751):

Congress shall make no law respecting an establishment
of religion, or prohibiting the free exercise thereof.

GERRYMANDER

Not everything produced by the Republican Generation was
so lofty. Two members of that generation devised a name for
a down-to-earth political principle still followed today, the
gerrymander.

It was named for Elbridge Gerry (born 1744), who in 1812
as governor of Massachusetts presided over a redistricting that
favored his party, the Democrats. The famous painter Gilbert
Stuart (born 1755), who was also a cartoonist for the Boston
Centinel, embellished a map of the new districts with the head,
wings, and claws of a dragon-like salamander. Editor Benjamin
Russell (born 1761) named it a *Gerrymander.* That name has been
applied ever since to the ubiquitous practice of redistricting elec-
toral maps to maximize advantage for the party in power.

THE COMPROMISE
GENERATION

(born 1767–1791)

After the great revolutionaries of what Strauss and Howe call the Republican Generation came a generation in their shadow, much as the Silent Generation followed the victorious G.I.s in the 20th century. Unlike the Silents, the Compromise Generation produced a plethora of U.S. presidents—seven in all—but at a time when the presidency and the national government were relatively weak. Instead, many of the Compromisers turned away from preoccupation with the Atlantic coast and busied themselves populating and civilizing lands to the west. They called themselves pioneers.

PIONEER

It was a military term, borrowed from French and used in the English language since the 16th century. In war, pioneers were foot soldiers (the word comes from Old French for "foot" or "pedestrian"). They were advance forces who prepared the way for an army on the move by clearing brush, building roads and bridges, and the like. In America, the word was adapted to civilian use. America's pioneers were not soldiers in an army but individuals who tamed the wilderness and brought American civil society with its laws and customs in their wake.

James Fenimore Cooper, himself a member of the Compromise Generation (born 1789), portrays them in his 1823 novel *The Pioneers, or The Sources of the Susquehanna*. It is set in the fictional town of Templeton in upstate New York, a place being transformed by pioneers, like its leading citizen, who muses:

> *The mind of Judge Temple, at all times comprehensive, had received, from its peculiar occupations, a bias to look far into futurity, in speculations on the improvements that posterity were to make in his lands. To his eye, where others saw nothing but a wilderness, towns, manufactories, bridges, canals, mines, and all the other resources of an old country, were constantly presenting themselves, though his good sense suppressed, in some degree, the exhibition of these expectations.*

Although Cooper admires "how much can be done, in even a rugged country, and with a severe climate, under the dominion of mild laws, and where every man feels a direct interest in the prosperity of a commonwealth, of which he knows himself to form a part," *The Pioneers* is far from an unqualified celebration of the advance of civilization. The main character is Natty Bumpo a.k.a. Leather-stocking, a man of the woods who advocates living with nature. At the end, Natty heads west:

> *This was the last they ever saw of the Leather-stocking. . . .*
> *He had gone far toward the setting sun—the foremost in*
> *that band of pioneers who are opening the way for the*
> *march of the nation across the continent.*

WILDERNESS

What the pioneers entered and eventually overcame was the *wilderness*—a term by no means unique to the Compromise Generation but one that occupied their thoughts as they steadily advanced the frontier westward in the 19th century. The American wilderness contained Indians and a few characters like Leather-stocking, who were content to live with nature rather than subdue it.

But subduing it was the principal concern. A reviewer in the *North American Review* of October 1830 recommends *Laurie Todd; or, The Settlers in the Woods* by John Galt as "a lively and correct description of the details of the process by which the 'woods are bowed beneath the sturdy stroke' of the adventurous emigrant, and the reign of civilization extended over the vast solitudes of the unexplored wilderness."

THE TRANSCENDENTAL GENERATION

(born 1792–1821)

After the Compromise Generation, according to Strauss and Howe, came the Transcendentals. In Strauss and Howe's 80-year cycle of generations, the Transcendentals following after the Compromisers were akin to the Boomers following the Silents in the next century. Like the hippies and flower children of the 1960s, the Transcendentalists questioned authority and received wisdom, established a commune, wore outlandish outfits, and believed in the basic goodness of Nature and of individuals free of government authority.

TRANSCENDENTAL

There was a name for this, one that they chose for themselves: *Transcendental*. That word, with its derivatives

Transcendentalism and Transcendentalist, wasn't new to the English language or to philosophy, but the New England Transcendentalists used it in a way distinct from that of philosophers on the other side of the Atlantic. Ralph Waldo Emerson (born 1803) was its leading proponent, arguing in his 1836 essay "Nature" for a spiritual relationship with Nature attained by solitude apart from human society. Others included Henry David Thoreau (born 1817), who actually "went to the woods to live deliberately." And in the 1840s Transcendentalists founded Brook Farm, an experiment in communal living that lasted seven years.

Like the hippie movement a century later, Transcendentalism didn't long transcend the generation that created it, but it lives on in American ideals of rugged individualism, distrust of government, and appreciation of nature.

O.K.

Meanwhile, in nearby Boston, another member of the Transcendental Generation bequeathed to the country its greatest and most successful word, one that was at the opposite pole from the lofty Transcendental ideals. The word was none other than *O.K.*, invented by Charles Gordon Greene (born 1804), founding editor of the *Boston Morning Post*. In the late 1830s Boston editors had amused their readers and themselves with humorous abbreviations like *R.T.B.S.* for "remains to be seen" and even better, the misspelled *O.W.* for "all right." On March 23, 1839, there appeared in the *Post* a complicated humorous story that ended with this sentence:

> The *"Chairman of the Committee on Charity Lecture Bells,"* is one of the deputation, and perhaps if he should return to Boston, via Providence, he of the Journal, and his train-band, would have the "contribution box," et cetera, o. k.—all correct—and cause the corks to fly, like sparks, upward.

It would take too long to explain exactly how this relates to a group of young men from Boston going by ship to New York City and getting the attention of the editor of the Providence, R.I., *Journal.* What matters is that this has the very first *O.K.*

We know it's the first, despite other claims for that honor, because it's so improbable that a joke misspelling would become a permanent addition to the vocabulary. *O.W.*, for example, never caught on. But two funny things happened to *O.K.* First, it was picked up a year later throughout the nation in the name of *O.K. Clubs*, supporting the presidential reelection campaign of Martin Van Buren, called "Old Kinderhook" because he hailed from Kinderhook, N.Y.

And then, also in 1840, a newspaper article claimed that Van Buren's predecessor Andrew Jackson was so illiterate that he would mark *O.K.* on a document when he approved it, thinking that was the proper abbreviation. The story was a hoax—Jackson was quite a good reader and writer—but the result was that within a few years, many people were writing *O.K.* on documents or telegraphing *O.K.* to mean that all was, in fact, correct.

By the early 20th century the joke misspelling was largely forgotten, and *O.K.* became pervasive in our conversation, if not in our formal writing. Nowadays it's the usual way to reach agreement: "Lunch at American Harvest?" "O.K." confirms agreement but refrains from value judgment like "Wonderful!" or "Oh, all right."

That's what makes *O.K.* so useful: It doesn't have elaborate connotations. And these days *O.K.* can be seen as encouraging tolerance, thanks to the well-known book title *I'm O.K., You're O.K.* It could even be argued that *O.K.* is the true American philosophy in a two-letter nutshell: We are concerned that things work, that they can and will perform well enough to keep things going, even if they are far from perfect.

THE GILDED GENERATION

(born 1822–1842)

Strauss and Howe name the next generation Gilded. Gilded indeed they may have been later in life, but first they had to pass the test of war.

SKEDADDLE

The Gilded Generation contributed to our vocabulary when they went to war. Particularly notable was a coinage that came from the first battle of the Civil War, a word in the newly exuberant hifalutin polysyllabic American pattern of *sockdolager* (something big), *absquatulate* (depart), *hornswoggle* (cheat), and *shindig*. The new word was, and is, *skedaddle*, meaning to scurry away, and it was applied to the Battle of Bull Run on July 21, 1861, where the defeated Union army beat a hasty and disorganized retreat back to Washington. Southerners called it the Great Skedaddle.

But it wasn't just the South who taunted the enemy with this ignominious word. When their forces retreated, they got the same label from the North. A month later, for example, the *New York Times* reported, "No sooner did the traitors discover their approach than they 'skiddaddled', (a phrase the Union boys up here apply to the good use the seceshers make of their legs in time of danger)."

A contemporary account of the Army of the Potomac, published in 1862, includes this comment on a battle that year:

> *A young officer of artillery, . . . belonging then to a detached corps of the C.S.A., . . . said in a hurried way,—* *"they will certainly be here to-night," and then . . . as he tapped his light grey uniform coat, "hadn't I better take this off and 'skedaddle' to Danville?"*

The word was put to use in verse too, as a rhyme in a poem celebrating General Lew Wallace, who held off the rebels in the siege of Cincinnati in 1863:

> *Who sat his prancing steed astraddle,*
> *Upon a silver-mounted saddle,*
> *And saw the enemy skedaddle? Lew Wallace.*

DEADLINE

Skedaddle was a way to make light of a serious business. There was nothing light in perhaps the grimmest of the newly coined war words, *deadline*. It was an actual line in the ground at a prison camp, or sometimes a fence. A prisoner who crossed the line would be shot dead. The notorious Andersonville prisoner of war camp in the South had such a line, as noted in a history of the war published shortly after it was over:

> *If my reader be shocked, as well he may be, at the above recital, let me assure him that I have not told him half the reality. I have said nothing of the punishments inflicted—the stocks, the chain-gang; nothing of the hospitals; nothing of the capture of fugitives and their rending by bloodhounds; nothing of the three hundred wretches shot for passing beyond the dead-line....*

An account of the trial in 1865 of the commander at Andersonville, Captain Henry Wirz, includes this report from an inspection after the war: "A railing around the inside of the stockade, and about 20 feet from it, constitutes the 'deadline,' beyond which the prisoners are not allowed to pass."

At the trial A. G. Blair, a New Yorker who was imprisoned at Andersonville, testified, "I have seen men on five or six occasions either shot dead or mortally wounded for trying to get water under the deadline. I have seen one or two instances where men were shot over the deadline.... I think that the number of men shot during my imprisonment ranged from twenty-five to forty."

This meaning of *deadline* continued well into the 20th century, as in the *Memoirs of a Murder Man* by Arthur A. Carey (1930):

> *Byrnes's murder cases were not the factors that built his fame. It was the effectiveness of his crime control system. He established the first police deadline when he sent a squad of picked men into the Wall Street financial section with orders to arrest every crook with a record who stepped across Fulton Street, which was the northern boundary of the financial and jewelry districts. For the first few months the deadline was established he paid the rent for the squad's office out of his own pocket. When he left the Police Department he was able to say that since he had established the deadline "not a ten cent stamp had been stolen in the section." The deadline exists to-day.*

But before that, at least by 1920, someone, likely a newspaper editor, had appropriated the deadly word for the modern sense of a time limit, perhaps in hope of intimidating reporters with dire consequences for failing to meet those deadlines.

THE PROGRESSIVE GENERATION

(born 1843–1859)

Strauss and Howe's grand scheme of generations following in orderly succession is disrupted—once—by the Civil War. Instead of a hero generation coming after the Gilded, the next generation they term artist; as children, members of this generation were "shell shocked by sectionalism and war," as explained in *The Fourth Turning*. "They came of age cautiously, pursuing refinement and expertise more than power."

One small segment of the Progressives pursued refinement so assiduously that they earned a new name for it.

DUDE

Dude! It's one of the great words of American English and surely the greatest contribution to our language by members of the Progressive Generation.

In 1882 *dude* was practically unknown. In 1883 it was on the pages of seemingly every newspaper in the United States, as a brand new label for a foppish young man. It burst on the scene thanks to a poem by a slightly older Progressive, Robert Sale Hill, an Irish-born resident of New York City who was 31 at the time. He introduced *dude* to the world on page 9 of the New York *World* of January 14, 1883, in an 84-line poem excerpted here:

The True Origin and History of 'The Dude'

The following "pome," somewhat inscrutable by THE WORLD,
is published as of probably interest "to whom it may concern,"
like A. Lincoln's Niagara letter to Horace Greeley:

Now lately in this hemisphere,
Through some amalgamation,
A flock of Dudes, I greatly fear,
Are added to our nation.

Their features, first I would explain
Are of the washed-out order——
Mild dissipation, feeble brain
With cigarette smoke border.

Their feathers o'er their brow they hang,
Their cheek resembles leather;
Their style, inclusive, is in slang,
The "Strike me with a feather."

Their father's cuff [collar] supports a hat—
The head just seen between them;
A coachman's riding coat at that
Envelopes all and screens them;

Save just below the coat is seen,
Where muscles ought to be, sir,
A pair of pipe stems, cased in green,
Skin-tight and half-mast high, sir.

To this please add a pointed shoe,
Verandas built around it;
A necktie, either white or blue,
C' est fini, if you doubt it.

They have their nests, also a club,
Alas, so misapplied, sir,
Like other birds they love light grub,
For beef's to them denied, sir.

They do not care for cruel sports,
Like foot-ball, cricket, gunning,
But lemonade they drink by quarts,
Their girling's "real stunning!"

Imported "dudes" are very shy
Now "Oscar's" [Wilde] crossed the ocean,
But native "Dudes" soon learn to fly
And seem to like the notion.

America can ill afford
To harbor such deformity,
And we would humbly thank the Lord
To spare us this enormity.

(It has been suggested that the "dood" pronunciation, and the idea for the word itself, came from the song *Yankee Doodle Dandy*. But that's just speculation.)

Starting in February of that year, other newspapers gleefully joined in the game, with columns of cartoons, poems, and prose. For example:

> *From the* New York Mirror *of February 24: "For a correct definition of the expression the anxious inquirer has only to turn to the tight-trousered, brief-coated, eye-glassed, fancy-vested, sharp-toes shod, vapid youth who abounds in the Metropolis at present. He is a Dood."*

From the *Brooklyn Daily Eagle* of February 25: "A dude cannot be old; he must be young, and to be properly termed a dude he should be one of a certain class who affect the Metropolitan theaters. The dude is from 19 to 28 years of age...."

From the New York *Evening Post* of March 3: "A dude, then, is a young man, not over twenty-five, who may be seen on Fifth Avenue between the hours of three and six...."

In 1883 Progressives were between 24 and 40 years old, Missionaries 23 and under. The majority of dudes, therefore, were born to the Missionary generation, but it was the Progressives who defined them.

Discussions of dudes weren't confined to Fifth Avenue in Manhattan. Researcher Peter Reitan has found articles in that inaugural year of 1883 in newspapers from Pennsylvania, Minnesota, Missouri, Kansas, Texas, Louisiana, Kentucky, South Carolina, West Virginia, Nebraska, Dakota territory, Washington state, California, and Hawaii. It was a rare example of an instant hit.

Dude has remained a powerful word ever since, but with quite a different spin Instead of mocking effete dandies, *dude* now is a term of respect for a real man. Theodore Roosevelt, born in 1858 near the end of the Progressive generation, may have been a major influence in this change. He grew up in a wealthy family in New York City and in the early 1880s dressed and looked like a dude. But he gained a different reputation by winning a bar-room brawl. And in 1884, after the death of his mother and his wife, he went off to the Badlands of the Dakota Territory for two years, no longer a dude in manners or appearance. For the rest of his life he kept busy as an outdoorsman, big game hunter, and Rough Rider.

Meanwhile, Westerners picked up *dude* as a term for city dwellers. For the rest of the 19th century *dude* remained pre-dominately pejorative, but picking up on the dude's aim for ele-gance the word morphed into the slang accolade it is today. It has developed somewhat like *guy*, except that *dude* remains mostly restricted to males. In the 1880s, excessively fashionable young women were sometimes called *dudines* or *dudettes*, but those terms have long since vanished.

A present-day example of *dude* comes in the Coen brothers' 1998 movie *The Big Lebowski*, featuring "the Dude," who at one point says:

> *Let me explain something to you. Um, I am not "Mr. Lebowski." You're Mr. Lebowski. I'm the Dude. So that's what you call me. You know, that or, uh, His Dudeness, or uh, Duder, or El Duderino if you're not into the whole brevity thing.*

CARPETBAGGER AND SCALAWAG

While the dudes were adjusting their finery, other members of the Progressive Generation packed their few belongings in a carpetbag and headed down from the northern states to ameliorate the conditions of ex-slaves and others in the defeated South. Or to make their fortune.

A carpetbag was a sturdy traveling bag made of scraps of carpet, popular at least as far back as the 1840s. Even before the Civil War it was associated with someone who traveled light, who carried his (or her) entire possessions in such a bag. A Kansas newspaper commented in 1857, "Early in the spring several thousand excellent young men came to Kansas. This was jokingly called the carpet-bag emigration."

These, like most of the men who fought in the Civil War, would have been from the previous Gilded Generation. But it was in the decade or so after the war that *carpetbagger* became a widely used term of opprobrium in the South, along with *scalawag*.

Scalawag was well enough known that it was an entry in an 1848 dictionary of Americanisms as "a favorite epithet in western New York for a mean fellow; a scape-grace." After the war white Southerners used it extensively as a companion for *carpetbagger*.

What was the difference? An interviewer in the 1872 *Report of the Joint select committee appointed to inquire into the condition of affairs in the late insurrectionary states, so far as regards the execution of laws, and the safety of the lives and property of the citizens of the United States and Testimony taken* asked an Alabama Democrat:

Question. You have used the epithets "carpet-baggers," and "scalawags," repeatedly, during the course of your testimony. I wish you would give me an accurate definition of what a carpet-bagger is and what a scalawag is.

Answer. Well, sir, the term carpet-bagger is not applied to northern men who come here to settle in the South, but a carpet-bagger is generally understood to be a man who comes here for office sake, of an ignorant or bad character, and who seeks to array the negroes against the whites; who is a kind of political dry-nurse for the negro population, in order to get office through them. . . .

Question. Having given a definition of the carpet-bagger, you may now define scalawag.

Answer. A scalawag is his subservient tool and accomplice, who is a native of the country. . . .

Question. Is scalawag regarded as a term of opprobrium?

Answer. Yes, sir; it is regarded as a term of political opprobrium, just as the term "bourbon," and "mossy-bank," and one term and another are politically opprobrious. [Those words stood for arch-conservative Southerner and arch-conservative Northerner, respectively.]

THE MISSIONARY GENERATION

(born 1860–1882)

HOT DOG

GALE: "What is the noblest kind of dog?"

MR. STRONG: "I give up."

GALE: "The hot dog. It not only does not bite the hand that feeds it; it feeds the hand that bites it."

That joke, published in *The Weekly Tribune* of Moulton, Iowa, in 1934 and recently rediscovered by researcher Barry Popik, is the kind of irreverent tribute accorded to the most American of foods ever since it acquired its irreverent name back in the 19th century.

The sausage that we now call a *hot dog* was originally, and still is, known more formally as *wiener* (from Vienna, Austria) and *frankfurter* (from Frankfurt, Germany). The dog part of *hot dog* came from another half-serious joke from as far back as the 1830s, asserting that the meat in these sausages came from stray dogs. For example, here's the *Boston Times* of September 18, 1831: "The Methuen gazette editor 'infers' that dog-meat sausages is a new article of food. Bless your soul man—it's as old as your granny."

As that century progressed, vendors began selling sausages heated up and served in a roll. And someone began calling the combination a *hot dog.* Exactly who it was, and where, and when, isn't yet known, but the increasing availability of historical newspaper databases has allowed researchers to get closer to the source. The name was new enough that it was making news in the 1880s and 1890s.

Currently the earliest known example of *hot dog,* rediscovered by Fred Shapiro, is from a detailed description in the *Nashville Tennesseean* in 1886:

> *"Hot stuff," "hot pup," "hot dog," sings out the fiend who carries in one hand a tin cooking arrangement, and on the other arm a basket. He is the wiener wurst fiend. It is his cries that greet you as you enter the theater and regreet you as you come out. He is the creature whose rolls make the night hideous, and whose wares make dreams that poison sleep.*
>
> *The luxury came originally from Austria. Wiener means little [actually, it means Vienna] and generally speaking, the purchaser gets a little the wurst of it. Wurst means, in English, sausage; so that when one of these*

> *peddlers says wiener wurst to you he means do you want a little sausage.*
>
> *The tin vessel which he carries is divided into two compartments. The upper is filled with water, in which are about a thousand, more or less, skin sausages. In the lower apartment is the alcohol stove that keeps the sausages hot. In the basket he keeps his rye bread and horse-radish. The sausage, sandwiched by two slices of bread which have been smeared with the horse-radish, make up the wiener wurst, which costs you a nickel.*

And from the Knoxville *Journal* the following September: "It was so cool last night that the appearance of overcoats was common, and stoves and grates were again brought into comfortable use. Even the weinerwurst men began preparing to get the 'hot dogs' ready for sale Saturday night."

Most of the other early sources for *hot dog* are from the Northeast. Here's the *Paterson* [N.J.] *Daily Press* of December 31, 1892: "Somehow or other a frankfurter and a roll seem to go right to the spot where the void is felt the most. The small boy has got on such familiar terms with this sort of lunch that he now refers to it as 'hot dog.' 'Hey, Mister, give me a hot dog quick,' was the startling order that a rosy-cheeked gamin hurled at the man as a Press reporter stood close by last night. The 'hot dog' was quickly inserted in a gash in a roll, a dash of mustard also splashed on to the 'dog' with a piece of flat whittled stick, and the order was fulfilled."

By the mid-1890s hot dogs were well known at colleges like Yale, where a "Kennel Club," also known as a "dog wagon," began making the rounds in 1894.

The inventor of the term *hot dog* might possibly have been "Hot Dog" Morris, a resident of Paterson, New Jersey, during the last two decades of an extraordinary life. An African American from Jamaica, Morris knew French and German and spoke English with a German accent. He had made a big salary traveling with a circus in Germany and Switzerland as a "wild man." In Paterson he opened a restaurant but later became a vendor of hot dogs.

Morris was born in 1838, a member of the Gilded Generation, but his involvement with hot dogs came during the younger years of the Missionary Generation, and so did the enthusiastic young consumers of hot dogs. We can credit the Missionaries with making *hot dog* a household world.

FAN

Enthusiasts of what was then our national pastime were known in the 19th century as *cranks, fanatics,* and beginning in the 1880s especially among members of the young Missionary Generation, *fans.* The word appears frequently in sportswriting, as in this early example found by researcher Barry Popik in the *Kansas City Times* of May 10, 1885: "I am more or less a base ball fan myself, and this reminds me that the man who is not thoroughly up on base ball slang nowadays is looked upon with pity. Of course a fan is a fanatic; that is simple enough to grasp."

In May 1886, *The Sporting News* reported, "The Boston fans explain the poor playing of their nine so far by saying that Radbourne does not get effective until June, while Buffinton has had a lame shoulder, Sam Wise has been sick and Burdock has been slow about getting down to work."

By 1901, an article on college slang could list "*fan*, n. A base ball enthusiast; common among reporters."

Ted Sullivan, a major league player, manager, team owner, and author, and a member of the Progressive generation (born 1851), gave himself credit for inventing *fan*. A 1907 article gives this account:

> *And who are the fans? This is a mooted question, even among the fans themselves; that is to say, the derivation of the word "fan" is not entirely clear. It is probably an abbreviation, and Ted Sullivan, who managed the St. Louis Browns in 1883, claims the honor of originating the term. According to Sullivan, a man entered the headquarters of his club one day, and started a conversation about baseball. The man was familiar with the names of every player of prominence in the country, and knew not only the percentages of the big clubs, but also the batting and fielding averages of the leading players. He had a decided opinion on every phase of the game, and was overanxious to express this opinion. When he had gone,*

> *Sullivan turned to his players and said: "what name*
> *could you apply to such a fiend as that?" Arlie Latham*
> *promptly replied: "He is a fanatic." "I will abbreviate*
> *that word," Sullivan responded, and call him a ' fan.' "*

Fan is such a natural abbreviation of *fanatic*, or indeed *fancy*
(boxing fans in England were called "the Fancy" throughout the
19th century) that it is likely *fan* was independently invented more
than once. Sullivan may indeed have invented *fan*, but so probably
did others. In any event, members of the Missionary generation
supplied enough fanatics for *fan* that it became the standard word
among future generations, not just of baseball fans but those of
any other activity or pastime.

SWEATSHOP

It was originally a technical term referring to an arrangement for
manufacturing clothing involving a middleman called a *sweater*.
It was Americans of the Missionary Generation, however, who
first used the term *sweatshop* for, in the words of the *Oxford English
Dictionary*, "a workshop in a dwelling-house, in which work is
done under the sweating system (or, by extension, under any system of sub-contract)."

Researcher Barry Popik once again has provided the earliest
example currently known, from the *Chicago Herald* in 1884: "A
custom tailor working as journeyman earns from $3 to $4 per

day; a girl in a tailor-shop known as a sweat shop, earns little more than that per week."

The *Chicago Tribune* in 1890 headlined: "In Darkest New York: Dreadful Places and Dreadful Things in the American Metropolis":

> *We must pass over his description of Jewtown and its sweat-shops, in which miserable Jews spend eighteen hours a day at slop-work for the clothing manufacturers, and from which clothing is often sent out leaded with the infection of small-pox and typhus.*

Thanks to the zeal of the Missionary reformers who advocated for laws to improve working conditions, by the early 1900s in American cities *sweatshop* had become more of a historical term, used mainly metaphorically to refer to other situations of extreme hardship.

THE LOST GENERATION

(born 1883–1900)

The generation born at the end of the 19th century, as early as 1883 and as late as 1900, became known as the Lost Generation in the aftermath of World War I. To their elders, and even sometimes to themselves, they seemed to have lost their way. What they really lost, however, was the previous century's values, attitudes, and language. This was the first generation to be *hip* and *sexy*, and to embrace the musical phenomenon called *jazz*.

The Lost Generation did not acquire its name until after the war and did so not in America but in Europe, when its members were young adults. A prominent member of the generation, Ernest Hemingway, chose for an epigraph of his 1926 novel *The Sun Also Rises*: "You are all a lost generation.—Gertrude Stein in conversation." Stein, in turn, credited the saying to the owner of a garage in Paris who scolded a young mechanic for belonging to a *génération perdue*.

Hemingway, Stein, and others like F. Scott Fitzgerald lost themselves comfortably in postwar Paris. Most Americans weren't so lucky. But many took their cue from the expatriates. Even back in the United States, the war had turned American mores upside down.

Nineteenth-century values still asserted themselves in the ratification of the Eighteenth Amendment to the U.S. Constitution in 1919, prohibiting "the manufacture, sale, or transportation of intoxicating liquors within, the importation thereof into, or the exportation thereof from the United States." But the enactment of *Prohibition*, a word going back to the Transcendental Generation, evoked counter-action and language to go with it, including *speakeasy* and *scofflaw*.

ADOLESCENT

Before they were Lost, members of this generation were the first to be widely viewed as adolescents, at least by pedagogues and the educated public. Not that the word was new; the *Oxford English Dictionary* finds it as far back as the 15th century. But it was rarely applied until the advent of the Lost Generation. To notice that young people went through a period of adolescence (boys 14 to 25 years old, girls 12 to 21, by one account) was to observe that it wasn't just a direct passage from child to adult. There was something special in between. The increased attention would result in the designation *teenager* two generations later.

In 1901 the *Proceedings of the Michigan Schoolmasters' Club* included this typical exhortation:

> *The changes in psychic power and function as manifested by unusual and sometimes abnormal activities are of such a character that they demand careful consideration, especially if the teacher hopes to profit by her study of the adolescent, and desires to benefit him by her knowledge of his nature. Psychologically he is often an enigma because of the conflicting and contending storm and stress of ideas as he is swayed to and fro, in his actions, by the overwhelming domination of the ever-changing emotions. . . .*
>
> *There is accelerated physical growth always accompanied by an increase of intellectual activities and intensified emotional interests. This has produced great results, as reference to the world's history will show. The world's work has been largely done by the adolescent.*
>
> *In this great intellectual awakening, characterized by the most intense altruistic feeling accompanied by increased love for nature, music, art and literature, these strong ideals have gone out in action that on the one hand, under the proper direction and sympathetic guidance of the intelligent teacher, has produced the master in science or art, or on the other hand, without this proper direction, the world's great criminals and insane.*

In 1913 and 1914, anthropologist Miriam Van Waters's dissertation, "The Adolescent Girl Among Primitive Peoples," was published in the *Journal of Religious Psychology*. She argued that restrictions on adolescent girls in our society drove some of them to criminal activity, while girls had more wholesome outlets in other societies. She cited case histories of young American women, including one who liked to dress in men's clothes and work as a laborer and was frequently arrested for vagrancy. "Compare treatment of this case with primitive treatment of the socially or physically inverted adolescent," she notes.

FLAPPER

But even as Van Waters was doing her research, an unanticipated antidote to restrictions on adolescent women was emerging in the form of the *flapper*.

The modern young woman of the Lost Generation began to style herself a *flapper* even before the generation was lost. A 1912 story in *The Saturday Evening Post*, for example, has a character simply called "The Flapper." This energetic young woman does many things, sometimes as simple as distracting her father from typing: "Bean murmured politely and began upon his letters. The Flapper was relentless. She sat in her father's chair and fastened the old look of implacable kindness upon him. He beat the keys of the machine. The Flapper was disturbing him atrociously."

In that same year the novels *A Flapper at School* and *Her Majesty the Flapper* were published. Among many other works of fiction, Janet Lee wrote *Wild Women: The Romance of a Flapper*, published in 1922, "A sprightly romance of a budding flapper (with an imagination) that prompted the English instructress to take a hand in the young lady's family affairs."

In 1925 the *New Yorker* published a cartoon with a sign in the background reading "The Wages of Sin" and this dialogue:

UNCLE: Poor girls, so few get their wages!
FLAPPER: So few get their sin, darn it!

Although the typical flapper was young, there was no restriction on age, as evidenced by a 1924 musical, *The Flapper Grandmother.*

Flapper could be a term of opprobrium. Frank Bartleman used *flapper* as an unflattering label for female ministers in a 1920 tract titled *Flapper Evangelism: Fashion's Fools Headed for Hell.* "Effeminate men follow a female ministry too largely through a spirit of fleshly attraction to the opposite sex," he wrote. "Because men will not obey God is the real reason for the general acceptance and popularity of flapper evangelism."

And there is disdain in *The Haunted Bookshop* by Christopher Morley, published in 1923: "You remind me of something that happened in our book department the other day. A flapper came in and said she had forgotten the name of the book she wanted, but it was something about a young man who had been brought up by the monks. I was stumped. I tried her with *The Cloister and the Hearth* and *Monastery Bells* and *Legends of the Monastic Orders* and so on, but her face was blank. Then one of the salesgirls overheard us talking, and she guessed it right off the bat. Of course it was Tarzan."

The Flapper Wife is a novel by Beatrice Burton, published in 1925. On the eve of her wedding day, the flapper muses: "A woman was either a slave or a doll. But if she was a slave, it was her own fault." To her mother she says: "Your idea of married life is to take care of your husband. Mine is that he is to take care of me! Where you ran a carpet sweeper I'm going to run an automobile!"

And in *Smoldering Flames* by Clara Palmer Goetzinger (1928): "What does the average girl get out of her flapper days unless she has money? Not much more than the eternal 'don't' and constant disappointments."

❧

A Flapper in Chicago

Ben Hecht, Chicago newspaperman and later author of *The Front Page,* gives a vivid account of a fictitious flapper in his 1922 collection of columns, *A Thousand and One Afternoons in Chicago.* The flapper is 18 years old, so technically she would be among the first of the next generation, carrying flapperdom to an extreme that might make her older sisters blush. He titled this sketch "Nirvana":

> *Then out of the babble of faces he heard his name called. A rouged young flapper, high heeled, short skirted and a jaunty green hat. One of the impudent little swaggering boulevard promenaders who talk like simpletons and dance like Salomes, who laugh like parrots and ogle like Pierettes. The birdlike strut of her silkened legs, the brazen lure of her stenciled child face, the lithe grimace of her adolescent body under the stiff coloring of her clothes were a part of the blur in the newspaper man's mind.*
>
> *She was one of the things he fumbled for on the typewriter—one of the city products born of the tinpan bacchanal of the cabarets. A sort of frontispiece for an Irving Berlin ballad. The caricature of savagery that danced to the caricature of music from the jazz bands....*
>
> *"Wilson Avenue," he thought, as he walked beside her chatter. "The wise brazen little virgins who shimmy and toddle, but never pay the fiddler. She's it. Selling her ankles for a glass of pop and her eyes for a fox trot. Unhuman little piece. A cross between a macaw and a marionette."*

Thus, the newspaper man thinking and the flapper flapping, they came together to a cabaret in the neighborhood. . . .

Above the music he heard the childishly strident voice of the flapper:

"Where you been hiding yourself? I thought you and I were cookies. Well that's the way with you Johns. But there's enough to go around, you can bet. Say boy! I met the classiest John the other evening in front of the Hopper. Did he have class, boy! You know there are some of these fancy Johns who look like they were the class. But are they? Ask me. Nix. And don't I give them the berries, quick? Say, I don't let any John get moldy on me. Soon as I see they're heading for a dumb time I say 'razzberry.' And off your little sugar toddles. . . .

"Say, I bet you never noticed my swell kicks." The flapper thrust forth her legs and twirled her feet. "Classy, eh? They go with the lid pretty nice. Say, you're kind of dumb yourself. You've got moldy since I saw you last."

"How'd you remember my name?" inquired the newspaper man.

"Oh, there are some Johns who tip over the oil can right from the start. And you never forget them. Nobody could forget you, handsome. Never no more, never. What do you say to another shot of hootch? The stuff's getting rottener and rottener, don't you think? Come on, swallow. Here's how. Oh, ain't we got fun!". . .

> She liked dancing and amusement parks. Automobile
> riding not so good. And besides you had to be careful.
> There were some Johns who thought it cute to play cave-
> man. Yes, she'd had a lot of close times, but they wouldn't
> get her. Never, no, never no more. Anyway, not while
> there was music and dancing and a whoop-de-da-da in
> the amusement parks.
>
> The newspaper man, listening, thought, "An infant
> gone mad with her dolls. Or no, vice has lost its humane-
> ness. She's the symbol of the new sin—the unhuman,
> passionless whirligig of baby girls and baby boys through
> the cabarets."

✄

SPEAKEASY

Flappers and their Johns went to *speakeasies*. As a name for a place
illegally selling alcoholic beverages, *speakeasy* had been around
since the late 19th century. But thanks to Prohibition, the speakeasy belongs to the Lost Generation.

The word is unusual enough that it evidently was a unique coinage, rather than a spontaneous invention by a number of individuals. In 1891, when the word was still new, the *New York Times* was
curious enough to send a reporter to Pittsburgh to track it down.
The reporter filed this story, published in the *Times* of July 6:

The Illegal Speak-Easies

Defiance of The Law in Pennsylvania.

Saloons in Which Beer and Whisky are Sold without License—How the Term "Speak-Easy" was First Applied to Them.

PITTSBURG, July 5.—The commonest item in the police news of Pittsburg is the raid of a "speak-easy." A speak-easy is an unlicensed saloon. In Pennsylvania it is the illegitimate child of the Brooks high-license law.

The term "speak-easy" is said to have originated in McKeesport, this county. Mrs. Kate Hester has for years been a saloon keeper there. She greeted the High-License act by defying it and continuing to sell beer without license. Her customers were a boisterous lot. When their conviviality became too noisy it was her custom to approach with warning finger upraised and awe-inspiring look and whisper: "Speak easy, boys! speak easy!" Soon the expression became common in McKeesport and spread to Pittsburg. Here the newspaper men accepted the term as filling a long-felt want. It now passes current all over the county as descriptive of a resort where strong drink is sold without license. Some day, perhaps, Webster's Dictionary will take it up.

✄

However it began, *speakeasy* is an odd word, and not a particularly charming one. As "Judgette" remarked in the magazine *Judge* in 1928, saying she had been "at a speakeasy for dinner which gave me another brilliant idea! The word Speakeasy is really terrible! Why doesn't someone invent a new name?"

Nevertheless, it was useful. For example, when Calvin Coolidge came to the presidency after the death of Warren G. Harding, Alice Longworth, daughter of Theodore Roosevelt, remarked about the change in the White House: "The atmosphere was as different as a New England front parlor is from a back room in a speakeasy."

Because speakeasies were illegal and not subject to licensing, there were no prohibitions against women or underage youths, no limits on hours of operation. A 1929 story in the *American Mercury*, "Murder in the Making" by Lawrence M. Maynard, illustrated the effects:

> *By the time Ev Drake was twenty-one and the rest of us were from sixteen to twenty, the speakeasy had come to take its permanent place among us. The old law no longer barred minors from saloons. The speakeasy, being an outlaw anyway, did not discriminate. A kid of fifteen could now buy a drink as easily as a man of forty. It was a new freedom for our gang. It was the beginning of our real career in crime. In the speakeasies we met older men*

> who were trained, not only in the arts of the racketeers,
> but in the more grim business of cutthroat competition,
> which meant the survival of the fittest, and rivals put
> out of the way.

In 1929 a political scientist argued, "Since Prohibition, for every saloon that has been closed there is either a still or a speakeasy or a bootlegger supplying the most vicious and injurious kind of liquor that it is possible to concoct or conceive of."

SCOFFLAW

Scofflaw was the winner in a contest sponsored by Delevare King, distinguished citizen of Quincy, Massachusetts, graduate of the Harvard class of 1895 and member of the Anti-Saloon League, to combat drinking with a word "which best expresses the idea of lawless drinker, menace, scoffer, bad citizen, with the biting power of 'scab' or 'slacker.'" On January 15, 1924, Mr. King proclaimed *scofflaw* the winner, chosen from 25,000 entries. It was sent in by two contestants, Henry Irving Dale of Andover, Massachusetts, and Miss Kate L. Butler of Dorchester, who shared his $200 prize.

And *scofflaw* indeed caught on, but for mockery rather than for repentance. Not for the first time a new word was stood on its head.

The *Harrisburg Telegraph* had a typical response:

✧

As to The New Word

> The scofflaw entered the scoffsloon. He leaned an elbow
> on the scoffbar and rested a foot on the scoffrail.
> "Whaddle'y' have?" said the scoffbartender.
> "A little tea," said the scofflaw.
> So the scoffbartender poured him something from a scoff-
> flask under the bar. It looked like tea.
> The scofflaw raised it; he scofflipped it suddenly.
> "How was it?" scoffed the scoffclerk of the scofflaw.
> "Scoffal," said the scofflaw, scoughing.

✧

The Albany *Times-Union* commented, "Scofflaw won't help much. What we need is dry agents who will scoff cash."

And Preferred Pictures promptly announced in the trade press its plan to make a movie, "The Adorable Scofflaw," "a story of a young dapper addicted to the cocktail habit."

SEXY

Until the 20th century, nobody was sexy. They may have been charming, seductive, enticing, but they weren't *sexy*. (In fact, they didn't even *have sex* until the 19th century.)

No, the generation that fought World War I and then fueled the Roaring Twenties was the first to be *sexy*. Or at least the first to put that word to use in a growing number of contexts.

We see it as early as 1908 in a review of *Handicapped*, a book not about a person with disabilities but instead about the son of a horse trainer, whose "heritage operates against him in matters of love." The reviewer in *The Nation* was unimpressed: "When the book is not horsy it is 'sexy.' It is also rather dull."

Sexy temptations, with "sexy" often in quotation marks, gave older generations concern for the young. In a 1918 book by "Captain X" telling of the training of American soldiers for the war in France, we read:

> *They like books—books about the war—you wouldn't think that? They devour them.... They like good stirring tales of adventure; a few went in for the sexy magazine story, all of which kinds of magazines we have since weeded out and refused admittance to the barracks—for obvious reasons. They like writers of the Robert Louis Stevenson, Richard Harding Davis type.*

Civilian youth too were at risk of having "sexy" experiences. Stephen Wise, rabbi of the Free Synagogue, wrote in a 1922 book about the vulgarizing and corrupting power of movies and plays: "But it is not enough for parents to censor the theatres frequented by their children and when they can to debar them from attendance at disgustingly 'sexy' plays. It is their business as far as they can to cultivate in their children the love of the best in letters and in the arts. It is not enough to call a halt to the pleasure-madness of our children."

There was no doubt that *sexy* could be found in the theatre. A 1922 issue of *Theatre Magazine* noted in a feature article on Helen Westley: "In Strindberg's *The Dancing Death*, Miss Westley was a wife, 'sexy, modern and neurotic,' as she herself described the role."

One of the *sexy* temptations was the pulp magazine *Snappy Stories*, whose full-color covers always featured, in the words of one researcher, "a beautiful, youthful white woman, generally in some various stage of seduction or undress." Nevertheless its editor announced in 1918, "*Snappy Stories* is departing from its previous policy of using risqué stuff—is in the market now for stories with 'punch,' but lacking anything in the least 'sexy,' as heretofore."

And in 1921 the editor of *Farm and Fireside* made a similar announcement: "We want good fiction for *Farm and Fireside*, and we will pay good money for it. The only kind we don't want is the extreme stuff—sexy-pink-tea and blood-and-thunder.

We don't demand a farm setting. Aside from that, we have no specifications."

Ben Hecht's 1922 novel *Gargoyles* includes a character expressing a dim view of the moralists: "The good clergymen and the statesmen and the welfare workers rushing into print with revelations of immorality are inspired by nothing more intricate than a desire for publicity, an ambition to pose before the public in the guise of fellow crusaders and civic benefactors. Their benefactions, you see, consist of offering the public lurid sex statistics over which it may gloat in secret. And in the meantime, over these benefactions, over these exciting sex statistics and sexy photos and over the people who discuss them and roll them over on their tongue, is thrown a protective fog of indignation."

Sexy was also in the air in the new science of psychoanalysis. Havelock Ellis's lengthy article "The Mechanism of Sexual Deviation" in a 1919 issue of *The Psychoanalytic Review* details "sexy" daydreams of male domination by a 28-year-old woman. "Florrie" had actually sent a letter to the editor of a newspaper telling of a suffragette being spanked for her presumption. It was pure fantasy, Florrie explained to Ellis, but it provoked considerable consternation in the press. "My only aim," Florrie told Ellis, "was to give myself a nice (as I now recognize) sexy feeling."

At other times she daydreamed of being slapped violently on the arm: "When he has finished with that arm he starts on the other arm, and then on her back until her skin is red all over, and at this point she experiences a 'sexy' feeling." Thinking of satyrs and nymphs in early Renaissance paintings, Florrie says, "I am quite sure that the nymphs liked the fauns and it gave them a lovely sexy feeling when a satyr dragged off an unwilling nymph. But it is only in day-dreams that the satyr-man exists."

In another daydream, Florrie is lying on the grass. A stranger "sits down by me and talks, but it rather passes over my head, for I feel that he is giving me a vague sexy feeling and I cannot resist it. He seems to know exactly how I feel, and sympathizes. . . . As each garment is removed I feel more and more helpless but more and more sexy."

Not all psychoanalysis was so sexy. A 1926 story in the *Century* magazine has an enthusiastic patient telling a friend that

> "the world is mine and that life is full to overflowing with beautiful things. Oh, my dear, you must go to my man!"
>
> "Does he ask you dreadful questions?" I suggested timidly.
>
> "No, indeed! He is not that kind of a person. He is not sexy, like Freud. Although," she added, "he is one of Freud's disciples. But he has moderated the great man's ideas to suit his own."

Over the past century, *sexy* has expanded its range from strictly sexual to more broadly exciting. People and clothing and actions can still be *sexy* in the plain sexual sense, but nowadays *sexy* can imply that anything is exciting, from food to furniture, from sexy pizza to sexy toasters to sexy accounting. Sexy also is something to celebrate, not to be censured or censored. *People* magazine, for example, every year celebrates *sexy* with its choice of "sexiest man alive." In 2014, that was Chris Hemsworth.

JAZZ

The famous baseball term *jazz*, introduced and embraced by the Lost Generation, became one of the biggest hits of the 20th century.

Baseball term? Yes, the evidence shows conclusively that *jazz* began, not in the clubs and halls of New Orleans, but in a ballpark in California.

The music we now know as *jazz* did indeed get its start in New Orleans. But the word was imported from California, via Chicago.

We know this thanks to the indefatigable research of Gerald Cohen, editor of the journal *Comments on Etymology*, and his collaborators. They have delved into every nook and cranny of the early 20th century in search of *jazz*, and what they have not found is as important as what they have found.

Here's what they have found, the very first instance in print of *jazz*. It's from the sports section of the *Los Angeles Times* of April 2, 1912:

Ben's Jazz Curve

> *"I got a new curve this year," softly murmured Henderson yesterday, "and I'm goin' to pitch one or two of them tomorrow. I call it the Jazz ball because it wobbles and you simply can't do anything with it."*
>
> *As prize fighters who invent new punches are always the first to get theirs Ben will probably be lucky if some guy don't hit that new Jazzer ball a mile today. It is to be hoped that some unintelligent compositor does not spell that Jag ball. That's what it must be at that if it wobbles.*

Henderson's *jazz* fizzled after that. A year later, however, it came back, again in a baseball context but this time in northern California. There it became the progenitor of the *jazz* we know today. The *San Francisco Bulletin* reported the return of the San Francisco Seals from spring training on March 6, 1913:

> *Everybody has come back to the old town full of the old "jazz" and they promise to knock the fans off their feet with their playing.*
>
> *What is the "Jazz"? Why, it's a little of that "old life," the "gin-i-ker," the "pep," otherwise known as enthusiasalum. A grain of "jazz" and you feel like going out and eating your way through Twin Peaks. . . .*
>
> *"Hap" Hogan gave his men a couple of shots of "near-jazz" last season and look at what resulted—the*

Tigers became the most ferocious set of tossers in the league....

The team which speeded into town this morning comes pretty close to representing the pick of the army. Its members have trained on ragtime and "jazz" and manager Del Howard says there's no stopping them.

The sound as well as the meaning of *jazz* would allow it to develop into America's second greatest homemade word, second only to the *OK* of the Transcendental Generation. It is only right that this great word should have been adopted soon afterward as the name of America's greatest musical phenomenon.

So *jazz* was invented in California. But how did it attach itself to the music phenomenon of the Lost Generation, one that had been called *blues* or *ragtime* or *rag*? The strongest evidence appears to be that it was brought from California first to Chicago. In the words of bandleader Bert Kelly, reminiscing some forty years later, "I conceived the idea of using the Far West slang word 'jazz,' as a name for an original dance band and my original style of playing a dance rhythm at the College Inn, Chicago, in 1914."

This *jazz* gave elders something new to worry about. It became a nationwide story in November 1916 when a dean at the University of Chicago forbade the use of drums by a "jass band" hired for a tea dance on campus. The *Los Angeles Times* picked up the story:

Because Miss Marion Talbot, dean of the girls, did not approve of the drum, that instrument was barred from

> the orchestra, and only a piano and the saxophones, the
> instruments composing what is called the "jass band"
> in the "black-and-tan" cafes, were allowed at the "hop"
> given by the Score Club.
>
> Miss Talbot is quoted as explaining: "It's not in keep-
> ing with the spirit of Ida Noyes Hall. The drum arouses
> all that is base in young people and tends to provoke
> immorality."

Finally, by 1916 *jazz* had arrived in New Orleans. The kind
of music known as New Orleans jazz had arrived much earlier;
only the name was imported from Chicago. The New Orleans
Times-Picayune of November 14, 1916, summed up the situation:

> Theatrical journals have taken cognizance of the "jas
> bands" and at first these organizations of syncopation
> were credited with having originated in Chicago, but
> any one ever having frequented the "tango belt" of New
> Orleans knows that the real home of the "jas bands" is
> right here.

And by 1917 *jazz* had swept the country. A Victor Records
catalog from March 1917 lists "The Original Dixieland Jass Band.
Spell it Jass, Jas, Jaz, or Jazz—nothing can spoil a Jass band. Some
say the Jass band originated in Chicago. Chicago says it comes
from San Francisco . . . across the continent."

PEP

Pep couldn't match *jazz* for expressiveness. But it too had a familiar place in the vocabulary of the Lost Generation. *Jazz* was an expansive and expressive word; *pep* was a little pop of energy, most likely derived from *pepper*. It too was originally a California baseball term, referring to "the 'jazz,' the pepper, the old life" needed for a team's success. The *Oxford English Dictionary* offers an even earlier baseball use, from August 1908: "Mighty little pep in the Giants' game today."

In 1914, the Reilly & Britton Co. of Chicago published a book by Col. Wm. C. Hunter with the title: *PEP: Poise—Efficiency—Peace: A Book of Hows Not Whys For Physical and Mental Efficiency.* He explains: "I have an abundance of PEP, which expressive little word stands for poise, pluck, peace, power, punch, patience, purpose, so far as P's are concerned, and PEP likewise means efficiency, enthusiasm, endurance, example and experience. PEP is the foe of worry and the friend of happiness."

In 1918, there was a *Soldier's Scrap Book: Full O' Fighting Songs and Poems with Pep.* In the same year, a book of *Poems of Pep and Point for Public Speakers.*

Rotarians relished *pep,* endorsing Col. Hunter's PEP program in their magazine and in a 1922 issue, for example, telling how to organize a glee club within a Rotary club: "The leader organizes a group of Rotary members as a vocal 'pep squad.' . . . Provided that capable leadership can be obtained, a glee club is easily organized from the 'pep squad.'"

A 1918 article in *The Drama* about Liberty Theatres created in training camps for soldiers remarks, "even where the professional visitors fail to show up—a rare occurrence—the 'pep squad' of trained soldier-amateurs are always ready to stage an impromptu show of their own."

Pep rallies also developed from *pep*, but they came into popularity among the Silent Generation in the 1940s.

HIP

The Lost Generation were the first to be *hip*. With the meaning "to be in the know," *hip* in turn became a legacy from the Lost to succeeding generations, who used it plain but also as a base for *hipster* (Silents and Millennials) and *hippie* (Boomers). A 1908 example from Jonathan Lighter's *Historical Dictionary of American Slang* has a character saying, "Oh, I'm so glad you got hip to yourself at last." So a present-day website can say of "the part-Catskills, part-cosmopolitan Lounge Kitty," "Yes, she's hip to the kitsch," with the same meaning for *hip*.

HEP

Around the same time as *hip*, and closely related to it in both form and meaning, *hep* too became a watchword of the Lost Generation. It could be just a spelling and pronunciation variant of *hip*. George V. Hobart's 1906 novel *Skiddoo* has an early example:

> *In that nerve-destroying moment I recollected my parting admonition to my wife when she went away, "Darling, remember, money is not everything in this world and don't write home to me for any more. And remember, also, that when the Jersey mosquito makes you forget the politeness due to your host, flash your return ticket in his face and rush hither to your happy little home in Harlem, where the mosquito never warbles and stingeth not like a serpent, are you hep?"*

23 SKIDDOO

As the Lost Generation began to move from adolescence to adulthood, they latched on to the newly developed phrase, *23 skidoo!* Its meaning is clear—Get out! Scram!—but its origins are not, providing a fruitful field for speculation. What does seem clear is that both *23* and *skidoo* by themselves also meant "Go away!" so that their combination was just an emphatic way of saying it. Researcher Barry Popik judiciously reports, "I have several articles that credit the vaudeville actor Billy B. Van with combining the two slang terms."

Skidoo is likely a variant on *skedaddle*, which had been around since the Gilded Generation used it in the Civil War. But *23*? Popik has found a plethora of theories expounded when *23* was new: it was the maximum number of horses allowed in a single race at English racetracks; it was used as a signal for a Mexican criminal arrested in New Orleans to escape; it was the number given to Sidney Carton at his execution in Dickens's *Tale of Two Cities*; it was 23rd Street in Manhattan, windy location of the Flatiron Building. That last couldn't be true, because Popik has found published examples going back to 1899, and the Flatiron Building was completed in 1902. Yet another proposal is that *23* came from telegraph code signifying "away with you!"

By the early 1900s *23 skidoo* had spread across the country, as evidenced by this item in *Walden's Stationer and Printer* for August 15, 1906.

∝

Pen Points

> "Twenty-three—skidoo!" has risen from a mere slang phrase to the importance of a national issue, for an association has recently been formed, whose purposes are "the abolition of a foolish superstition and the exaltation of the name of skidoo." The association's name is "The Sons of Skiddoo," and the first requisite of membership is that the applicant's birthday occurs the twenty-third of the month. Its success was instantaneous and already protests are pouring in that the "daughters" have been needlessly neglected. Although bravely setting out to combat what they style "a pernicious habit," the leaders show their dormant fear by giving vent to the expectation that

the reply of the general public is likely to be formulated
by one word—"Skiddoo!"

That year also F. Kelly's novel *Man with Grip* included this dialogue: "As for Belmont and Ryan and the rest of that bunch, SKIDOO for that crowd when we pass." And later: "I can see a reason for 'skidoo'," said one, "and for '23' also. Skidoo from skids and '23' from 23rd Street that has ferries and depots for 80 per cent of the railroads leaving New York."

And for four cents, as an ad in *Collier's Weekly* said that year, you could buy a "23 SKIDOO" badge.

Finally, also in 1906, Mrs. Leslie Holdsworth's song "Skiddoo! Skiddoo!! '23' for You!!!" was published. The second of its five verses goes like this:

(Girl) *My father was an orator of very high degee.*
(Boy) *Skiddoo! Skiddoo! Twenty-three for you!*
(Girl) *His keeper always spoke of him as number twenty-three.*
      Skiddoo! Skiddoo! Twenty-three for you!
      He revised the Constitution so it read a diff'rent way
      And took it to the President in Washington one day.
(Boy) *They put him in the daffy house and there he'll have to stay!*
(Together) *Skiddoo! Skiddoo! Twenty-three for you!*

SLACKER

Slacker is a name often applied, sometimes with pride, to certain members of Generation X. But it has a prominent prehistory.

It was applied with some admiration to college students, at least at Oxford. "You may not know what a slacker is," writes a Harvard man from Oxford in an 1898 issue of *Harper's Weekly*:

> *and if I should go to the pains of defining the word, you would probably say that it applies to all English undergraduates. But the true slacker avoids the worry and excitement of breakfast parties and three-day cricket matches, and is more apt to conserve his energies by floating and smoking for hours at a time in his favorite craft on the Char.*
>
> *He is a day-dreamer of the day-dreamers; and despised as he is by the more strenuous Oxford men, who yet stand in fear of the fascination of his vices, he is as remote and appealing a figure to the average American as a negro basking on a cotton wharf. Merely to think of his uninterrupted calm and his insatiable appetite for doing nothing is a rest to Occidental nerves, and though we may never be roustabouts and loaf on a cotton wharf, we may at any time go to Oxford and play through a summer's day at being a slacker.*

But it acquired a different meaning during World War I. When Johnny of the to-be-Lost Generation went off to fight the Germans, men who stayed behind were called *slackers*. An article titled "Penny Slackers" in *The International Steam Engineer: Official Journal of the International Union of Steam Engineers* for January 1918 declares:

> The war has developed numerous kinds of slackers, a term by the way, which seems to have found its origin in the way and was first applied to the men who sought to escape military service.
>
> The term slacker, as applied to a man who seeks to escape military duty, is one of contempt. The public has come to look upon such a man as a coward,——a man who not only lacks patriotism, but the element of personal courage; and it is probably true that many a man has enlisted voluntarily to escape being called a slacker.

The article also castigates "dollar slackers" who won't buy Liberty Bonds, and the "penny slacker," who won't buy Thrift Stamps.

In 1917, Jewell Bothwell Tull published *The Slacker: A Play in One Act*, written for the Philomathean Literary Society of Cornell College, Mt. Vernon, Iowa, and produced by them in November 1917. In this play, *slacker* is the ultimate insult. Grant Moore, age 32, feels obliged to stay with his mother and his fiancée instead of joining the Army. A neighbor, Mrs. Ralph, says, "If I were a man

I wouldn't let two women, who are able to take care of them-selves, make a slacker out of me! . . . Grant Moore's nothing but a slacker, and I said so! He's big and strong and his mother's got a pension and this house and enough besides to keep her the rest of her days."

Betty, his girlfriend, tells Grant, "They're saying you are—oh, that horrid word!"

Grant replies, "A slacker? Well—I suppose it can't be helped. They'll have to say what they please, but I've got to do what I feel is my duty." Fortunately at the end he decides it's his duty to enlist, and he avoids "that horrid word."

THE G.I. GENERATION

(born 1901–1924)

On June 27, 1936, when members of the generation that succeeded the Lost were between 12 and 35 years old, President
Franklin Delano Roosevelt laid a load on their shoulders.
Accepting the nomination for his second term in a speech to
the Democratic National Convention, he weighted them with
responsibility for their times. At the end of his long oration, he
declared, prefiguring the argument of Strauss and Howe: "There
is a mysterious cycle in human events. To some generations much
is given. Of other generations much is required. This generation
of Americans has a rendezvous with destiny."

And the weight of the world did seem to descend on the new
generation as the depressed 1930s wore on, only to be replaced
by World War II.

True, Roosevelt wasn't exactly thinking of 12-through-35-
year-olds when he gave that speech. In that bleak time he wasn't
exempting the Lost Generation, born 1883–1900, or his own
Missionary Generation, the youngest of whom, including

Roosevelt himself, were born in 1882. (And in his convention speech he sounded like a missionary, proposing faith, hope, and charity as guiding principles.) Still, more than any other 20th-century generation, those we now label the G.I. Generation had to face the greatest challenges.

They had begun their adulthood happily enough, the boys mostly too young to serve in the First World War, the girls mostly old enough to become flappers during the Roaring Twenties, and both to follow the footsteps of the Lost into the speakeasies, where there was no age minimum. But then their troubles began. The youngest of them missed the fun and excitement of the Jazz Age entirely, and the whole generation suffered the brunt of the Depression.

At the beginning of the 1930s, the flappers of the Roaring Twenties danced out, and at the end the G.I.s marched in. Those of that generation who missed the first world war became the soldiers (and sailors and pilots) of the second. And demonstrating that they were indeed a heroic generation, according to Strauss and Howe's scheme, in that war they prevailed. Little did they or President Roosevelt know it when he presented his challenge in 1936, but a decade later, having bravely faced dangers seen and unforeseen, after their war they would be called by some the Greatest Generation.

G.I.

When men of this generation became soldiers in the 1940s, they became *G.I.s*. Their soldier predecessors in the Gilded

Generation of the Civil War had the nickname *doughboys*, and in the Lost Generation of World War I soldiers were also known as *Yanks*, even if they came from the South. In World War II sometimes *doughfoot*, derived from *doughboy*, was used for soldiers. But in general, and for the first time, *G.I.* caught on as the preferred term.

During the First World War, *G.I.* was in fact rattling around in the military, but with entirely different meanings. It was a military abbreviation for "galvanized iron," and that led to the nickname *G.I. can* for a large artillery shell. Jonathan Lighter's *Historical Dictionary of American Slang* has several examples from 1918: "Their artillery sent over shot after shot of G.I. cans," "A G.I. can full of mustard [gas]," "Our first air raid was experienced last night.... Several G.I. cans were dropped at Royaumeix."

But as that war came to an end, *G.I.* was also reinterpreted as "government issue," and thus it came to refer not just to galvanized iron but also to other items issued to soldiers. It was therefore only a slight extension of meaning to use *G.I.* as a term for the soldier himself, and that was what happened in World War II. Lighter's slang dictionary notes that G.I. was used especially in journalism, perhaps because it was unpretentious, perhaps also because it was conveniently brief for headlines.

G.I. became a verb too. The *American Ski Annual* in 1941 explained, "To 'G.I.' a floor, you simply take government issue soap and government issue scrubbing brushes." And *G.I.* was the inspiration for a poem that was widely circulated in several

versions, always addressed to a sweetheart back home. Here is a
version attributed to one Howard C. Turner:

Here I sit on my G.I. bed,
with my G.I. hat upon my head
My G.I. pants, my G.I. shoes,
all is free, nothing to lose,
G.I. razor, G.I. comb,
G.I. wish that I was home.

They've issued me everything I need,
paper to write on, books to read,
My belt, my socks, my G.I. tie,
all are free, nothing to buy,
They issue me food that makes me grow,
G.I. wish I were on furlough.

I eat my food from a G.I. plate,
and buy my needs at a G.I. rate,
It's G.I. this and G.I. that,
G.I. haircut, G.I. hat.
Everything is G.I. issue.
Oh, darling, G.I. miss you.

Another version has these lines:

At night my G.I. prayers I say,
To win our G.I. peace some day,

And when this G.I. war is through,
Then G.I. will return to you.
Now G.I. stands for government issue,
And my darling, G.I. miss you.

The soldier himself was sometimes called *G.I. Joe*. "Government Issue, GI. How simply a technical term becomes part of our speech," wrote Rose Pesotta in a 1944 book. "Daily I read letters and hear from my co-workers about GI Joe, and others."

This *Joe* evoked some controversy, thanks to Damon Runyon. In "The Brighter Side," his syndicated column for January 9, 1945, Runyon imagined himself appearing before a judge:

Q. And what was your contribution to the war effort, Mr. Runyon?
A. I never called him G. I. Joe. . . .

Q. Would you mind stating your reasons for never calling him G. I. Joe?
A. I always considered the term with reference to its more familiar connotations in American city talk, in which for over forty years a Joe has meant a Jasper, a Joskin, a yokel, a hey-rube, a hick, a clod-hopper, a sucker. . . . I did not think it dignified. As a matter of fact, I thought it silly.

Q. . . . Did you ever speak of him as dogface or doggie or doughfoot or doughboy?
A. I did not.

Q. Well, then, would you please inform the court what you did call him?
A. Soldier.

In response to that attitude, as *Time* magazine reported in its issue of February 5, 1945: "Folks at home began to feel embarrassed. Almost since the war started, they had innocently used the term 'G.I. Joe.' Then from Santa Barbara, Calif., came a report that soldiers resented it, thought it patronizing. Hearst Columnist Damon Runyon gave his old-soldier version of the name.... Runyon remembered that in the last war G.I. (i.e., 'government issue') meant 'the big galvanized iron garbage and ash can in the back of each company barracks.' Other columnists and letter writers took up the protest."

It was the *Joe* that bothered Runyon. No such possible stigma was attached to *G.I.*

ACRONYM

We live in a world of *acronyms* nowadays, but it wasn't always so. It took an "alphabet soup" of initials and words constructed from them during the New Deal of the 1930s and the world war that followed to bring about that technical term.

G.I. was just one of many examples. The New Deal had the CCC (Civilian Conservation Corps), NRA (National Recovery Administration), REA (Rural Electrification Administration), and WPA (Work Projects Administration), to name a few.

A 1944 issue of *Word Talk*, published by the G. and C. Merriam Company of dictionary makers, notes the abbreviation proliferation in an article titled "Acronym Talk, or Tomorrow's English." Examples of World War II abbreviations in that article include

PT (Patrol Torpedo) boat, LST (Landing Ship Tank), and QMC (Quartermaster Corps), as well as SNAFU (Situation Normal, All Fouled Up in the sanitized version).

Other World War II abbreviations include endless U.S. government agencies: OCD (Office of Civilian Defense), ODT (Office of Defense Transportation), OPA (Office of Price Administration), OWI (Office of War Information). Women of the G.I. generation joined the WAC (Women's Army Corps) or its Navy equivalent the WAVES (Women Accepted for Volunteer Emergency Service). Radar too was a development of World War II—Radio Detection and Ranging, as it was named in 1940.

GUNG HO

It's not an old Chinese proverb, but it is Chinese. In that language, *gung ho* means something like "work peace." It was a designation used by the Chinese Communist government for industrial cooperatives, and it would have remained just that if it were not for a member of the Lost Generation (born 1896), Colonel (later General) Evans Carlson of the U.S. Marine Corps. In the late 1930s, he was a military advisor with the Chinese Communists in their fight against the Japanese. Carlson understood *gung ho* to mean the command, "Work together!" And he brought it into English by using it as a motto for the Marines of the G.I. Generation under his command in World War II.

In 1942, Carlson and his "Gung Ho" battalion of Marine Raiders attained fame with a raid on Japanese-held Makin Island intended as a diversion from the fighting in Guadalcanal. His Raiders then went on to Guadalcanal and fought behind enemy lines for a month. The exhortation "Gung Ho" soon spread far and wide with news of his success and the help of a feature film in 1943, " 'Gung Ho!' The Story of Carlson's Makin Island Raiders," starring Randolph Scott and Robert Mitchum.

Carlson told *Life* magazine in 1943: "My motto caught on and they began to call themselves the Gung Ho Battalion. When I designed a field jacket to replace the bulky and orthodox pack they called it the *Gung Ho* jacket. And they named every new thing *Gung Ho*."

To *Liberty* magazine that same year he explained: "Finally we adopted *gung ho* as a yardstick. Any action was *gung ho* or it wasn't. To help a man out of a tight spot, to jump in and do anything that needed doing without asking whose turn it was to do it—that was *gung ho*."

Gung Ho quickly found civilian use. A widely repeated story in an industrial publication of 1943 explained: "Long ago, the Chinese with their genius for co-operation posted on trees and buildings these symbols, 'Gung Ho.' 'Gung,' 'together' or 'common.' 'Ho,' 'peace,' 'happiness,' 'working.' 'Gung Ho'— 'Working together.'

> *Two years ago, a Wyman-Gordon worker told this little story at a shop gathering, and soon thereafter "Gung Ho" began appearing on walls and machines, here and there in our shops.*

Since then, *Gung Ho* has continued to be used to describe someone extremely enthusiastic, sometimes overly enthusiastic. Until the 1970s the expression generally used capital letters, but since the 1970s the preferred spelling has been *gung ho.* Perhaps credit should be given to Boomers for the switch to lower case, which shows the term's increasing acceptance as an ordinary English expression, but the G.I.s deserve the honor by being *gung ho* in word and deed.

BOYFRIEND AND GIRLFRIEND

Before depression and war, the later-to-be G.I. Generation had its frivolous days in the Roaring Twenties. In the generation's earlier years, the world was disarming and the country was prospering, and this younger generation could go about the business of being young. For some that meant imitating their big sisters as *flappers*, but more and more they rejected that extreme of rebellion. *Boyfriend* and *girlfriend* were words first used in their modern sense by this generation, and they show its character: simple, wholesome, direct.

In the early 20th century, a *boy friend* was a friend who happened to be a boy, and a *girl friend* was a friend who happened to be a girl. Later generations removed the space before *friend*, making *boyfriend* and *girlfriend* unequivocal terms for committed romantic relationships. But for the G.I. generation, boys and girls still could be just friends.

For example, a story in a 1920 issue of *Cosmopolitan* (the same Cosmo sexified in 1965 by Helen Gurley Brown) uses *girl friend* in this sense of a girl or woman who is friends with another. A "cigar-stand girl" says to a man, "Oh, I guess everything's nice and smooth just now. I seen m' girl friend yesterday, and Gus was taking her to the movies last night, so I guess everything's nice and smooth."

A 1922 issue of *The Family Journal of Social Casework* discusses 16-year-old Mary, whose "girl friend" (the author used quotation marks for the term) was a bad influence: "She and her 'girl friend,' with several boys, would go to a cheap vaudeville or to the friend's house where questionable petting parties ensued."

More wholesomely, in the 1930 Nancy Drew *Mystery at Lilac Inn*, we find "They were now entering the business section of River Heights. Jean asked Nancy to let her off in the center of town. 'I'm going to the optician's first. Then I'll go to my girl friend's.'" For women referring to women friends, it's a meaning that remains today.

But we can see the modern meaning of *boy friend* and *girl friend* emerging alongside the older one in a 1921 story for young people, *The Corner House Girls Among the Gypsies*, one of the Corner House Girls series for young readers. Two preadolescent girls, Tess and Dot, have a neighbor friend named Sammy. "Why, Sammy is just like one of the family," says Dot, and the book calls him "their boy friend" several times.

But they also have an older sister Agnes (or Aggie), "the flyaway sister," and she has a "boy friend" in the modern sense, Neale O'Neil:

> *Neale O'Neil appeared just then to answer to the summons of his girl friend. He had been to the store, and he tumbled all his packages on Con's bench to run out into the yard to greet Agnes.*

Likewise, Faith Baldwin's 1931 novel *Skyscraper* uses *girl friend* in both senses:

> *"You live alone?" asked Lynn, looking about. "It's very attractive."*
>
> *"No, I've a girl friend—she's a model, too, but over in the regular wholesale district—coats and suits," explained Jennie. "Want a drink? I've got some gin."*

Later, Lynn thinks to herself "it would be pleasant to have a friend, a *man friend*, an older man upon whose cool, impersonal strength one might lean when things became too difficult for one." And *man friend* becomes the modern *boy friend* later in the book:

> *"How's the new boy friend?"*
> *"Boy friend?" Lynn's eyes were wide.*
> *"Drop the lashes over the baby stare. Dwight, the lad who gets 'em out of the hoosegow, for a price."*
> *"Oh, he's a dear," said Lynn wholeheartedly.*

An overview of this well-behaved new generation can be found in a special report in the June 5, 1938, issue of *Life* magazine, "Youth Tell Their Story." One such youth is Kenneth James, 18, who lives with his parents in a suburb of Baltimore. We are told that he likes swing music, radio, and politics:

> *He has a pleasant bedroom, three $15 suits, a $65 car just bought and driven by a girl friend until he gets a license. When he grows up—say 26—he wants to get married, have three children and be a radio announcer or a Republican politician.*

Prohibition ended in 1933, but "Kenneth neither smokes nor drinks nor wants his wife to do either."

"The ice-cream parlor is the universal rendezvous of U.S. youth," *Life* continues in a photo caption. "Here is Kenneth in Read's drugstore having sodas with his girl friend (right) and his girl friend's girl friend."

"Whether they live in the city or the country, have jobs or go to school, American youth has two common denominators," *Life* says. "The first is reading the funnies.

> *The second . . . is its love for the neighborhood candy shop or drugstore. Here "cokes," pops and soda are perennial favorites.*

But elsewhere in that issue we read about Europe on the brink of war, soon to enlist millions of these funnies-reading, drugstore-dating young people in matters of life and death.

CHUM

Another term in vogue for this wholesome generation was *chum*. With *boy friend* and *girl friend* there could be some ambiguity about the relationship, but *chum* was comfortably free of any implication of romance. You can find *chum* in in many of the book series for young people, such as the 1912 book *The Flying Girl and Her Chum* by L. Frank Baum (yes, author of *The Wizard of Oz*), one of the Flying Girl series. The "flying girl" Orissa Kane never refers to a *girl friend*, but twice she talks about her *chum*:

> *Sybil Cumberford is my best chum. The description still applies, so far as the airs and eyes are concerned; but the child is a young lady now, and a very lovable young lady, her friends think.*

And later: "My chum, Sybil Cumberford, has made several short flights with me; but Sybil's head is perfectly balanced and no altitude affects it."

Still later the narrator comments: "To wade in the warm, limpid water of the Pacific, at a place far removed from the haunts of humanity, in order to propel the precious craft on which her life and that of her companion might depend, to a better location, seemed to this girl quite the natural thing to do. Sybil's acute sense of humor led her to recognize the laughable side of this queer undertaking; yet even Sybil, much more frail and dependent than her beloved chum, had no thought of refusing her assistance."

Popular Mechanics for March 1927 has a short report with *chum* in the headline:

> *Girl Models Chum in Cement*
> *As Garden Ornament*
> *As a mark of esteem for her girl friend, a young woman*
> *in Illinois modeled her portrait in cement and set it upon*
> *a slender pedestal in the garden. She took the idea from*
> *Lorado Taft's statue of "Blackhawk" on the cliffs of the*
> *Rock river.*

Perhaps the most famous *chum* of all, however, was the fictitious Chet Morton. In the first Hardy Boys story, *The Tower Treasure*, he is introduced on page 6 as their "school chum." On the next page we learn that "he was a plump boy who loved to eat and was rarely without an apple or a pocket of cookies." And "his round, freckled face" soon becomes familiar in story after story.

NECKING AND PETTING

Not all boy friends and girl friends were just friends, as we have seen. Sometimes they were closer. In that situation, when boys and girls of the G.I. Generation expressed affection for each other, they generally indulged in *necking* and *petting*, intimate activities that stopped short of full sexual intimacy. *Necking* involved face-to-face closeness, *petting* body-to-body.

F. Scott Fitzgerald has a section titled *Petting* in his sensational 1920 novel, *This Side of Paradise*. An 18-year-old, Amory, discovers "that great current American phenomenon, the 'petting party.'"

> *The same girl... deep in an atmosphere of jungle music and the questioning of moral codes. Amory found it rather fascinating to feel that any popular girl he met before eight he might quite possibly kiss before twelve.*

Babbitt, in Sinclair Lewis's 1922 novel of that name, "had heard stories of what the Athletic Club called 'goings on' at young parties; of girls 'parking' their corsets in the dressing-room, of 'cuddling' and 'petting,' and a presumable increase in what was known as Immorality."

Here are a young woman's thoughts in John Dos Passos's 1925 novel, *Manhattan Transfer*:

> *Suppose I'd gone with that young man with the ugly necktie who tried to pick me up.... Kidding over a banana split in a soda fountain, riding uptown and then down again on the bus, with his knee pressing my knee and his arm round my waist, a little heavy petting in a doorway.*

Among college students, petting and necking seem to have become the norm in this generation. A 1929 book, *Sex in Civilization*, by two authorities with the imposing names Victor

Francis Calverton and Samuel Daniel Schmalhausen, says as much: "It is certain that at present the sex problem with which the college authorities have to deal is not so much complete and normal sexual intercourse as certain more juvenile substitutes and approximations, such as petting or necking."

Interviewed for a survey in 1931, a college woman told how one thing led to another:

> *My roommate during my sophomore year mocked contin-*
> *ually and finally I started in, just to keep her company.*
> *Now a cigarette is apparently a necessity. Whether or*
> *not I could stop I don't know, I never have tried. "Heavy*
> *petting," so-called, was not in the accepted code at all,*
> *in my younger days. And the change was not sudden, by*
> *any means. But I found out that if I permitted the boy*
> *I thought I was going to marry certain liberties during*
> *vacation periods when I see him, that it was much easier.*

SWELL

" 'It's a swell suite,' whispered Jordan respectfully," when she and Nick and Daisy and Tom and Gatsby took a suite at the Plaza on a hot summer afternoon in F. Scott Fitzgerald's 1925 novel.

"And as soon as we can afford it we'll take a real swell apart-ment, with an elevator and a telephone girl," Olive says to Merlin in Fitzgerald's 1922 story, "O Russet Witch!"

Swell was well known on both sides of the Atlantic even in the 19th century, but the generation born in America in the first part of the 20th century took it to new heights. It became a cause for complaint from language guardians like Howard Roscoe Driggs, who wrote in *Our Living Language: How To Teach It and How To Use It*, published in 1921: "Those given to the over-use of slang generally have, after all, only a few expressions to cover a multitude of ideas. With them, for example, every unusual thing may be swell; as, 'a swell party,' 'a swell automobile,' 'a swell dress,' 'a swell dish of ice cream,' 'a swell day.'"

Another example is the purported writing of a young miscreant known as Stubby Jenks in a book of that name by Donald J. Howard, published by the *Altoona Tribune* in 1921. Stubby is a boy of about 12, and Soffie is 11:

> *The reazon why Mary Ellen can have her old Party for all I care and I aint a bit Interrestid is becauze I got a Invitashun to a Swell Party Myself and its to be a Maskerade and the one thats havein it is Soffie Wingate and im to be the main Guy at the Party which aint strange becauze she thinks im jest about rite which she aint for rong if I do got to say it Myself, and maneys the Time I give her a Swell big Appel or a Sower Ball or Sumthing Good and when I wuz at Bostun I sent her a Swell Post Card with Shiney Stuff on it that cost a Nickel and it wuz so Ellegant that you wuzzent jest Suppozed to put a Stamp on it and Male it but you had to put it in a Envellope and send it.*

When men of the G.I. Generation put on their uniforms and went to war, they took the comfort of *swell* with them to the corners of the earth, using it plentifully in letters home. No, the war wasn't swell, but their friendships were.

Lt. Harry Dowd Jr., an Army Air Force pilot stationed in Algiers, wrote to his new wife in Chicago on Christmas Day 1942: "I am well and had a swell turkey dinner today at the Officers mess but gosh I would have loved to have been able to sit alongside of you.... I received letters from ICom written as late as Nov. 19th yesterday and they were sure a swell Christmas present."

In January 1943, he wrote to his family in Chicago: "It was sure swell seeing Dan, Bob and all the other fellas again and they were all glad to see me. Bob Palenscar started hollering hello and what not while he was still a block away and you'd have thought I'd been gone for ten years the way he acted. They're sure a swell gang." Two months later he died in his P-38 fighting German aircraft over Tunisia.

SWING MUSIC

What's that swing that Duke Ellington sang about in his 1932 song, "It don't mean a thing if it ain't got that swing"? *Life* magazine, spotter of trends, explained in its November 1, 1937, issue, "Hot jazz, or swing music, has in the last couple of years become a raging U.S. cult of which 28-year-old Benny Goodman (left) is generally recognized as the high priest. Consequently, the Madhattan [*sic*] Room in New York's Hotel Pennsylvania is a nightly scene of wild adulation where intermittent dancing and dining is subordinated to the almost scholarly pleasure of listening to Benny 'feel his stuff.'

"LIFE takes you herewith to the Pennsylvania on a recent Saturday night when some 375 couples, many of them fresh from the Columbia-Pennsylvania football game that afternoon, crowded into a small dance room, gladly paid the $1.50 cover charge to listen to the disciplined vagaries of Mr. Goodman on the clarinet, Gene Krupa on the drums, Teddy Wilson on the piano. Mr. Goodman and his perspiring men blended brass, reed and percussion while couple after worshipful couple, mostly of college age, gathered enraptured before the bandstand or sat at tables moaning their appreciation of the hottest passages—in the jargon of swing music, *whacky*."

Just two and a half years later, again according to *Life* of December 18, 1939, swing was becoming passé. "Glenn Miller is 28. When he played alongside Benny Goodman eleven years ago, Miller's 'slip-horn' was as hot as a stovepipe. But today, young America is turning away from swing music. The jitterbugs are forsaking the 'gutbucket' boys. They want their music sweeter and simpler. Glenn Miller plays more sweet numbers than hot. His greatest success has been with the 'juke boxes,' the nickel-in-a-slot automatic phonographs. Miller is easily the most outstanding juke-box artist of 1939. Among non-sweet bands, Benny Goodman is still the most popular."

Around that time Ellington himself (born just two years too early to be in the G.I. Generation) explained: "No notes represent swing. You can't write swing because swing is the emotional element in the audience and there is no swing until you hear the notes. Swing is liquid, and though the same group of musicians may play the same tune fourteen times, they may not swing until the fifteenth time."

JITTERBUG

Harlem bandleader Cab Calloway, a member of the G.I. Generation (born 1907), invented the *jitterbug* in 1934. At first he used it in lyrics to describe the jitters associated with drinking. His vocal that accompanied his Cotton Club orchestra in the fast *Jitterbug* music began like this:

> *If you like to be a jitterbug*
> *First thing you must do is get a jug*
> *Put whisky wine and gin within and shake it all up,*
> *And then begin.*
> *Grab a cup and start to toss;*
> *You are drinkin jittersauce.*
> *Don't you worry you just mug*
> *And then you'll be a jitterbug.*

But a year later he used it as the name for a kind of jazz dance or dancer. The name was spread throughout the country in the short movie called "Cab Calloway's Jitterbug Party," with lengthy and fast lyrics:

Listen all you chillum to that voodoo moan,
There's a modern villun worser than that old boogie woogie,
When that goofy critter spot your fancy clothes,
He injects a jitter,
Starts you dancing on a thousand toes,
There he goes.
Who's that hiding in the tree top?
It's that rascal The Jitterbug
Should you catch him buzzing 'round you,
Keep away from The Jitterbug.

For the benefit of readers far from Harlem, *Life* offered an explanation in its issue of May 16, 1938: "Jitterbug dancing is what the word suggests. The whole body seems to be in a jitter, the knees are continually bouncing and the only thing that does not enter into the Jitterbug movement is the facial expression."

ZOOT SUIT

What to wear at the dance? One extreme was the *zoot suit*, described in a popular song of 1941. A guy says:

I want a zoot suit with a reet pleat
And a drape shape, and a stuff cuff
To look sharp enough to see my Sunday gal.

And a gal replies:

> *You want a reef sleeve with a right stripe*
> *And a rare square, so the gals will stare*
> *When they see you struttin' with your Sunday pal.*

The gal, in turn, explains:

> *I want a brown gown with a zop top*
> *And a hip slip, and a laced waist*
> *In the sharpest taste to see my Sunday man*
> *A scat hat and a zag bag*
> *And a slick kiss, so the other chicks*
> *Will be jealous when I'm with my Sunday fan.*

A reef sleeve, a zop top, who knows? Just so many words. There really was such a thing as a *zoot suit*, however, though the explanation in the song is more rhyme than reason. It was an ostentatiously oversized men's suit with a long jacket, long pants with a high waist and tight at the cuffs, and a prominent watch chain. The song was popular, but actual zoot suits were more limited in their appeal, a kind of anti-fashion worn mostly by minority young men, especially African American and Chicano.

It is said that the first zoot suit was made to order in Gainesville, Georgia, in February 1940 and pictured in *Men's Apparel Reporter* a year later, with resulting interest around the country. Nobody has accounted for the name *zoot*, however.

DOGGIE BAG

Not every member of the G.I. generation went off to war, but those who stayed home were involved in the war effort too. That included rationing of everything from sugar to gasoline to meat. People were encouraged to grow vegetables in "victory gardens" in their yards and to feed dogs with table scraps rather than purchased dog food. Under the circumstances, when dog owners ate at a restaurant, it wasn't much of a stretch to think about bringing some of the meat home to feed the dog. Taking food from a restaurant wasn't proper in those days, so diners would be inclined to smuggle the meat home in a napkin. And so to prevent loss of napkins, or perhaps to encourage patriotic frugality, some restaurants began offering a carton or a waxed paper bag for the meat.

As the idea spread, restaurateurs came up with names like "Pet Pakits" and "Bones for Bowser." By the 1950s, however, *doggie bag* had become the generally accepted term.

For a while, the practice itself remained a breach of etiquette. Indeed, there was some suspicion that people without dogs were taking food home for their own use. "I do not approve of taking leftover food such as pieces of meat home from restaurants," Elizabeth Post, another member of the G.I. Generation (born 1920), snipped in her etiquette column in 1968. "Restaurants provide 'doggy bags' for bones to be taken to pets, and generally the bags should be restricted to that use." She relented soon after, however, saying in 1975, "Now, with the cost of food and the enormous proportions in the restaurant, and the starvation in the world, you just hate to see waste."

SENIOR CITIZEN

One lasting accomplishment of the G.I. Generation was to be first to be accorded respect as *senior citizens.* The term goes back at least to the 1930s, but it was only in the 1970s, when the oldest members of that generation were in their seventies, that the new expression for "old people" was widely applied.

Researcher Barry Popik found a 1929 newspaper announcement from a "Senior Citizen's Association" in Appleton, Wisconsin. He also found California politicians using the term in 1937 and 1938, in particular in a *Los Angeles Times* column by Frank Kent:

> *WASHINGTON, Oct. 27.——One of the major developments in American politics, frequently commented on in recent months, is the multiplicity of new schemes for granting and increasing pensions to the aged—or, as some politicians are tenderly beginning to call them, "our senior citizens."*

Was it an unctuous euphemism or a term of respect? In the 1930s, the words came from politicians who might be seen as pandering to older constituents. But decades later, when the G.I.

Generation was being looked on as the Greatest and was beginning to enter old age, *senior citizen* was a label they might comfortably accept, along with the respect of a grateful nation.

The label "greatest generation" was more or less permanently affixed to the G.I. Generation in Tom Brokaw's 1998 book of that name, where he declared, "it is, I believe, the greatest generation any society has ever produced." Brokaw was the first to use capital letters for the label. But he was far from the first to make that judgment.

In *Generations*, Strauss and Howe remark, "The expression 'senior citizen' is so much a part of our modern vocabulary that we forget how new it is—and how it did not come into wide use until the first peers of these seven G.I. presidents [Kennedy through G.H.W. Bush] started to reach old age. As with every other life phase, G.I.s have infused old age with uncommon collective energy."

SENIOR MOMENT

But the senior citizens had their senior moments too. In the 1990s, they were the first to recognize it. Emily Whaley of the G.I. Generation, in her 80s in the '90s, addressed the situation with humor in her 1997 book, *Mrs. Whaley Entertains: Advice, Opinions, and 100 Recipes from a Charleston Kitchen*:

> *I had a visitor in the garden last week, a delightful gentleman who, when searching in vain for the right word, said of his lapse of memory, "I'm having a senior*

moment." Now there is a piece of wisdom I'm certainly glad to have, for I have many such moments myself. My parents taught me this: You will be given as much as you give. My visitor with his "senior moment" gave me a new and very handy phrase at the same time that he was reassuring both himself and me that we are not alone in the world.

A year later, the American Dialect Society recognized this new term as the Most Euphemistic word or phrase of 1998.

THE SILENT GENERATION

(born 1925–1942)

Entering adulthood during the years of prosperity after World War II, the generation born between 1925 and 1942 came under scrutiny from their elders, and the elders were concerned. The concern wasn't that they were rebellious, but the opposite.

These are my people. I'm just barely old enough to be a member of what Strauss and Howe call the Silent Generation. And I remember well that the authors of *Generations* were far from first to label us that way. Back in the 1950s when we were just beginning to reach adulthood, our reticence earned us that designation. At college in the 1950s, I can remember laments by our elders that ours was a self-absorbed generation uninterested in politics and world affairs. Maybe so.

Time magazine was apparently responsible for giving our generation its name. In November 1951, a *Time* cover story declared:

> The most startling fact about the younger generation [defined here as ages 18 to 28] is its silence....

> *By comparison with the Flaming Youth of their fathers*
> *and mothers, today's younger generation is a still, small*
> *flame. It does not issue manifestos, make speeches or*
> *carry posters. It has been called the "Silent Generation."*

Time said the youth of the Silent Generation were "grave and fatalistic," "conventional and gregarious." "Perhaps more than any of its predecessors, this generation wants a good, secure job.... Today's generation, either through fear, passivity or conviction, is ready to conform."

Putting it another way, a reader responded to that article, "Never before has a generation been subjected to so many admonitions, accusations, reminders, analyses and lectures from its parents, graduation speakers, employers and newsmagazines. In fact, it's just possible that the younger generation is not silent at all—merely drowned out."

Time's concern was echoed by many, and thus by consensus, even by our own admission, forever after we were known as the Silent Generation.

ORGANIZATION MAN

William H. Whyte Jr. characterized college students of this generation in his 1956 book *The Organization Man*. "Whatever their many differences, in one great respect they are all of a piece: more than any generation in memory, theirs will be a generation of bureaucrats."

GRAY FLANNEL SUIT

Tom Rath, *The Man in the Gray Flannel Suit* of Sloan Wilson's 1955 novel, became the example and image of the organization man. Early in the book, preparing for a job interview at United Broadcasting Corporation in Manhattan, "Tom put on his best suit, a freshly cleaned and pressed gray flannel." There he interviews with Mr. Everett, "a man about Tom's age and . . . also dressed in a gray flannel suit. The uniform of the day, Tom thought. Somebody must have put out an order."

Rath is a member of the G.I. generation, born in 1920 and a veteran of World War II, but he symbolized the future the Silents supposedly were aiming for. When they got older, the Silents married and settled down, the husband to work for a corporation and the wife to be a suburban homemaker. Or so the ideal seemed to be in the 1950s.

Commencement speakers found our silence a convenient theme. "Arise, Ye Silent Class of '57," *Life* commented in June of that year: "Seldom had a graduating class come in for so much keel-hauling by the orators, who seemed to feel that many of the Class of '57, unlike the gobbling rebellious young turks of the past, were a silent generation—perhaps even prefabricated 'organization men' only too eager to claim faceless and voiceless roles in a world whose besetting sin was unprotesting conformity. The conformity by the orators was a demand for revolt against conformity. Their exhortation, far from being 'Disperse, ye rebels!' was more an almost anguished plea to 'Rebel, ye dispersers!' "

In short, we of my generation weren't Lost, and we weren't heroic. We were just relatively quiet, especially compared with the world-saving G.I. Generation that came before us. The Boomers that followed us also proved to be anything but silent. Strauss and Howe point out that our generation was unique in never managing to produce a U.S. president, although Jimmy Carter, born 1943, came close. We had other things in mind.

True to their nature, this generation really didn't worry about what their elders called them. For the most part we were silent about that Silent label, or at least unconcerned. We were too busy discovering ourselves as teenagers, the first generation to do so. It was a major shift in American culture. In terms of their historical significance, those born 1925–1942 could be called the Teenage Generation.

TEENAGER

Who put the bomp in the bomp bah bomp bah bomp? Who put the ram in the rama lama ding dong?

The Silents did, that's who. They were the first to recognize themselves as teenagers, with all the rights and privileges thereto pertaining.

Nowadays upon turning thirteen a young person is acutely aware of entering a special phase of life: a phase shared by neither children nor adults. It is not a phase to hurry through with the aim of becoming a grownup as quickly as possible, but one to savor for its own culture, its own fads in music, clothing, language, and attitudes. For that view of the teenager you can thank the Silent Generation.

It might seem as if there have been teenagers forever, because there always have been people between the ages of thirteen and nineteen. The term *adolescent* had been in use for that age group by members of the Lost Generation, in reference to others, not themselves. But not *teenager.* The notion of a special "teen age" is barely a century old.

It wasn't young people who first thought to make the teen ages special. Instead, apparently it was pedagogical and religious authorities who first used the terms *teen, teen age*, and *teenager.* They used them as they took note of the distinctive attitudes of persons aged thirteen through nineteen, more with worry than with approval.

In the Google Books collection we can find early instances of *teen* and *teen age* in the *Proceedings of the Thirty-Seventh Annual Session of the Minnesota Educational Association Held in Saint Paul, Minnesota December 26, 27, 28, 1899.* Those proceedings include a talk by John N. Greer, principal of Central High School in Minneapolis:

> *Boys and girls in their teens! What a problem in psychology and child study is represented by these words! How little of it is written or yet understood! They are not men and women, nor yet are they children. They typify the period when hope and fancy and ambition grow apace. To them the future is grand and attractive, and to be easily conquered. Self-consciousness is just blossoming. Egotism is in luxuriant bud. The mind discriminates not between the liberty and the license of thought. Mental generalizations and deductions are rampant. The young mind will rush in and have that 'perfectly at home' feeling, where in later years it will as readily conclude that only angels dare enter.*

And later: "The teen age is the imaginative age and not much given to reason and judgment. The reins of community government are not safe in the hands of any save mature and experienced minds."

In the same vein, in 1914 in the journal *Religious Education* a worrier declared: "The Bible School has many problems. Among them the keenest of these is the teen-age boy. How to hold him in the Bible School is the great question that is facing pastors, superintendents and teachers on every hand."

And the *Methodist Year-Book* 1921 tells about Epworth School for Girls in St. Louis, "a Christian home and school for delinquent and incorrigible girls of teen age."

From *teenage* to *teenager* was only a short jump, but it wasn't until the 1940s that we begin to see it in print. It was then that the Silent Generation to be, the younger brothers and sisters of those who went off to fight World War II, found themselves labeled *teenagers*.

In a 1942 book, *The Organization and Operation of the Oklahoma High School Athletic Association*, we read, for example: "The teenager is looking for thrills, and in contact sports there is a thrill on every play."

When the term *teenager* was introduced, it continued to emphasize trouble. A 1943 magazine article begins: "Curfew never rings out in St. Petersburg, Fla., for no curfew law is needed to keep the teen-age girls off its teeming streets at night—teeming with thousands of handsome young servicemen in the local Army Air Force Replacement Center. No curfew law is needed for there is a legal ordinance which gives the police the power to keep the teenager off the streets unless she is accompanied by a guardian or parent, or if she is on a legitimate errand."

During the first half of the century, seen from the outside, the teen years were times of trouble both for the teens and for the adults who had to deal with them. But the Silent Generation began reinterpreting the teenage experience. As more and more teenagers went to high school, that became the focus of distinctive teenage culture.

Life magazine took a snapshot of girls in Webster Groves, an upscale St. Louis suburb, in its December 11, 1944, issue: "Teen-Age Girls: They Live in a Wonderful World of Their Own":

> *Some 6,000,000 U.S. teen-age girls live in a world all their own—a lovely, gay, enthusiastic, funny and blissful society almost untouched by the war. It is a world of sweaters and skirts and bobby sox and loafers, of hair worn long, of eye-glass rims painted red with nail polish, of high-school boys not yet gone to war. It is a world still devoted to parents who are pals even if they use the telephone too much. It is a world of Vergil's* Aeneid, *second-year French and plane geometry, of class plays, field hockey, "moron" jokes and put-on accents. It is a world of slumber parties and the* Hit Parade, *of peanut butter and popcorn and the endless collecting of menus and match covers and little stuffed animals.*
>
> *It is also a world of many laws. They are capricious laws, changing or reversing themselves almost overnight. . . . Months ago colored bobby sox folded at the top were decreed, not by anyone or any group but, as usual, by a sudden mysterious and universal acceptance of the new idea. Now no teen-ager dares wear anything but pure white sox without a fold. She must not let a beauty parlor do her hair, nor can she wear heavy make-up, too-long fingernails, a hat, stockings or high-heeled shoes.*

She must not drink, must not neck with boys she does not
know well and, above all, she must never do anything too
grown-up or too sophisticated.

BOBBYSOXER

The legacy of the Silent Generation is still with us in the persons of teenagers. But each generation manifests its teenagers in different ways. For one thing, their looks have changed. And for the Silent Generation, the way teenage girls dressed made such an impression that they were known as *bobbysoxers*.

The name came from the *bobby socks* the girls wore, beginning in the 1930s. These were ankle-length white socks, called "bobby" perhaps because they were "bobbed" or short. Sometimes girls wore the tops of the socks straight up, sometimes folded over, depending on local fashion. With the socks the girls typically wore saddle shoes or penny loafers and full skirts. For girls, bobby socks were a visible badge of their status as teenagers, different from children and adults.

And the difference wasn't just in the way they dressed, but the way they behaved, especially in groups. Bobbysoxers were to be found not only at school but at Frank Sinatra concerts. When young Sinatra performed at the Paramount in New Jersey on December 30, 1942, the place was packed with bobbysoxers. As Sinatra later recalled, "When I came around the corner in a taxi and saw the marquee with my name on it I was knocked out. The sound that greeted me was absolutely deaf-ening, a tremendous roar. Five thousand kids, stamping, yell-ing, screaming, applauding. They let out a yell and I thought the roof would come off. I was scared stiff. I couldn't move a muscle. Benny Goodman froze too. He turned around, looked at the audience and said, 'What the hell is that?' I burst out laughing."

Comedian Jack Benny introduced Sinatra at that performance. In his words: "I thought the goddamned building was going to cave in. I never heard such a commotion with people running down to the stage, screaming and nearly knocking me off the ramp. All this for a fellow I never heard of."

And Bob Weitman, manager of the Paramount, recalled, "there were about 5,000 people in the theater. And all 5,000 were of one voice, 'F-R-A-N-K-I-E-E-E-E-E-!' As they danced in the aisles and on the stage, the loge and the bal-cony swayed. One of the managers came over to me and said, 'The balcony is rocking. What do we do?' We struck up the National Anthem."

The hysteria wasn't entirely spontaneous. A friend of Sinatra's publicist later explained, "We hired girls to scream when he sex-ily rolled a note. The dozen girls we hired to scream and swoon did exactly as we told them. But hundreds more we didn't hire screamed even louder. Others squealed, howled, kissed his pic-tures with their lipsticked lips, and kept him a prisoner in his dressing room between shows at the Paramount. It was wild, crazy, completely out of control."

Four years later, the atmosphere was as intense as ever. A writer for *Billboard* reviewed a Sinatra performance at the Paramount on November 7, 1945:

> *Current show is Frank Sinatra all the way. No matter what he did, whether it was a song, a piece of business or an ad lib, the bobby-sox bansheed like crazy. Fact that the singer is the emcee and is on stage practically all the time, except when other acts do their numbers, didn't detract from his appeal. It was "our Franki-e-e-e" from the time the bandstand came up until it went down.*

BOBBY-SOX BRIGADE

To be a bobby-soxer in the 1940s was to be cool. Shirley Temple, then aged 19, was one, at least in a movie. She was the bobby-soxer in the 1947 comedy *The Bachelor and the Bobby-Soxer*. In that movie the bobby-soxer gets a crush on a G.I. Generation bachelor, played by Cary Grant (age 43), but is cured from her infatuation in time to step back and allow the bachelor to romance her grown-up sister, played by Myrna Loy (age 42).

But to be a bobby-soxer in the 1940s also conveyed a threat of menace to adults, expressed in the term *bobby-sox brigade*. *Newsweek* of March 6, 1944, reported: "In New York City last week, the 'Bobby-sox Brigade' had swelled to such alarming proportions (within a year the Wayward Minors' Court had had nearly 100 per cent increase in delinquent-girl cases) that police imposed an unofficial curfew." And the *Lincoln* (Nebraska) *Evening Journal* on March 22, 1944, reported, "Police in Hartford, Conn., are on the alert for members of the 'bobby socks brigade'—girls of school age found loitering around drug stores, taverns, military installations, movies, and railroad and bus terminals."

The phenomenon of teenage girls going wild at performances of young male musicians began with the Silent Generation and has continued to the present day. But by the 1960s when the Boomers became the teens, bobby socks and bobbysoxers were passé. After the 1950s no teenager would consider herself a bobbysoxer, any more than she'd be a flapper.

BABYSITTER

Another innovation bequeathed to successive generations by the teenage Silents was the *babysitter*. In previous generations, adolescent girls had taken care of younger children in their own families, or families of relatives and neighbors, but babysitting was something different: a professional service, for pay, caring for children regardless of personal connections. With fathers away and many mothers working during World War II, the demand for babysitters greatly increased.

Their pay at first was 25 cents an hour, later 50–75 cents, and that enabled babysitters, mostly girls, to buy clothes, cosmetics, magazines, and movie tickets, thereby asserting their distinctiveness as teens. *Life* magazine, always alert to trends, explained in a 1949 article: "A baby-sitter with a steady trade can make more than $10 a week. This she can spend as she sees fit. If she is normal she will squander some of it on vanilla Cokes, the newest Montgomery Clift movie, a recording of *I Never See Maggie Alone* and save some for skates and a portable radio. She will thus have about $5 left for clothes."

At first there was uncertainty about what to call them. They were *mother's helpers, neighborhood helpers*, and *child minders*, but in the early 1940s the two words *baby sitter* and then the compound *babysitter* gradually became the norm. *Babysitter* was a less sentimental and more accurate term; the babysitter's primary responsibility was to sit at home, hour after hour, till the parents came back. As the earlier names implied, mother's helpers had generally been expected to help with household chores, but babysitters saw their role as just being there in the parents' absence, minding the children only as needed. With the children in bed, it was rumored, babysitters sometimes used the telephone to invite friends over and party, to the consternation of concerned parents.

Miriam Forman Brunell wrote in her 2009 book *Babysitter: An American History*:

> During the 1950s the "bobby-soxer babysitter," who "raided the icebox and jitterbugged with the crowd, until Mommy and Daddy arrived after midnight to discover Junior sailing boats on the bathroom floor" dwelled in the imagination of middle-class adults anxious about the

potential of teenage girls to disorder their living rooms and disrupt their lives.

The "bobby-soxer babysitter" concealed another troubling reality: while the vast majority of teenage girls worked as babysitters, many felt as ambivalent about babysitting as did those before them.... Devising an innovative vocabulary, sitters expressed their dislike of the "supercharged" baby boomer "brats" they were hired to watch, the male "wadders" who ripped them off, and the stifling suburban "babyvilles" in which they lived.

JUVENILE DELINQUENTS AND JUVES

When the bobbysoxers were bugging their elders with shrieking, swooning, and jitterbugging, or were off babysitting, what were the boys up to?

With their elder brothers off fighting World War II, all too many of the younger generation, it appears, were in danger of becoming juvenile delinquents. They were nicknamed *juves*, as in this article from *Billboard* of March 4, 1944:

> Civic Groups Bid for Hot Licks to Distract Bobby Socks Following N.C. Lead:
> 　L.A. Station Finds Juve Club Remote Helps
> 　Civic groups all over the country are bidding for hot musical groups to distract juves.

> *Object, of course, is to divert their attention from dirt
> and drink to manners and minding....*
>
> *KGPJ, Los Angeles, reports that records of top orks
> [orchestras] are being used by the station in an attempt
> to change the juve delinquents into jive darlings....*
>
> *KOFJ broadcasts from the Boys' Club of Hollywood
> the first "Junior Night Club" remote. The night club is
> for teen-agers from 14 to 18 and was organized to curb
> juvenile delinquency.*

The concern about delinquency was more a matter of image than reality. A 1960 study of a working-class suburb noted, "The extent, for example, to which the *impact* of juvenile delinquency upon the public consciousness depends not on criminal acts, but on long sideburns, rock and roll, motorcycles, and black leather jackets is worth some research."

RHYTHM AND BLUES

As the Silent Generation came of age, racial segregation and discrimination in the United States was at its height. But the sobering experience of World War II, where the United States fought against seriously evil empires with strong notions of racial superiority, led to the beginnings of more equitable treatment for African Americans. One byproduct was the term *rhythm and blues*, at first occasionally *blues and rhythm*, applied beginning in

1948 in place of *race music* to designate popular music by black artists. It was still segregated, but "race" was no longer part of the label. And soon enough R&B became a principal ingredient in the new transracial music phenomenon known as:

ROCK AND ROLL

No wonder the Silent Generation didn't produce any presidents. When they were young, they were too busy being teenagers. And the later Silents were present at the birth of *rock and roll*.

Cleveland, Ohio, is the present-day home of the Rock and Roll Museum. Not coincidentally, Cleveland is where the Silent Generation began to adopt a new kind of popular music and a name to go with it: *Rock and roll* to be formal, or *Rock 'n' roll* as it was said. During 1951 disk jockey Alan Freed, calling himself "Moondog," applied that term to the black rhythm and blues music he played on Cleveland radio station WJW in what he called "Moondog Rock 'n' Roll Party." Looking back in 1960, a *Time-Life* book on *This Fabulous Century* described rock and roll as "a thundering mixture of country-western music with Negro rhythm and blues."

The music recently renamed R&B had been popular in the black community, but Freed was the first to play it for an increasingly enthusiastic audience of young white listeners. He also sponsored the first rock and roll concert, the Moondog Coronation Ball, at the Cleveland Arena on March 21, 1952. The concert exceeded expectations, drawing twenty thousand listeners to an auditorium holding only ten thousand. It had to be stopped an hour after it began, with the excluded crowd breaking in. That just made for greater popularity, however, and rock and roll soon swept the nation, once again causing consternation for parents of the Silents.

GOING STEADY

But despite their alarming taste in music, the Silents remained true to the conservative social style inherited from their older sisters and brothers of the G.I. Generation. In fact it was the Silents who made *going steady* the ideal, if not always the norm, for teenagers. For many Silents, having a secure dating partner was better than being loose and free, "playing the field."

Going steady was already a fact of life in a 1946 play, *The Inner Willy*, by Bettye Knapp. Willy asks sixteen-year-old Carol for a date, and she replies: "Oh, it's sweet of you to ask me, Willoughby, but I can't.... You see, I'm going steady now.... For two weeks already. Everybody is going steady these days, you know."

Here's a daughter speaking with her mother about *going steady*, from Joyce Ingalls's 1953 *Teen Talk: Sixteen Character Sketches for Teen-aged Girls and Boys*:

> *I've got to decide if Jim is the man I want to go steady with. And I have to know before I go steady if I'm in love with him because we might get engaged or married or*

> *something—and even if we shouldn't, I couldn't go out with any other boys.*
>
> *You went out with other boys, and Dad went out with other girls! But Mother, you might have lost out, loaning him around like that. No one ever does that any more.*

A 1953 study of dating patterns at the University of Wisconsin, reported in *Family Life: Sourcebook* by Oliver Byrd (1956), found a "going steady complex" desired by many students for many reasons: security, peer pressure, avoiding "fiercely competitive" random dating: "Going steady is a means of providing a degree of 'date security' or 'participation insurance' to those who practice it."

And *Senior Scholastic*, the high school magazine, in 1956 declared: "What you think about going steady is enough to fill 52 issues of this magazine! Most of you seem to be for it, but there's a powerful minority against it! You all agreed that it doesn't necessarily lead to the altar."

In 1959 *Ladies' Home Journal* worried: "Most of the adult world is opposed to young teenagers' going steady. 'They get too intense about it,' say worried parents. (It isn't easy to remember what an intense time adolescence is, once you have passed it.) Children in their early teens ought to be having fun, getting to know people—lots of people, not just one. Psychiatrists have called going steady 'a conformist relationship.' The Catholic Church regards it as 'pagan' and at least one spokesman has expressed the view that teen-agers who go steady too young are 'slaves of their own making.' "

TRICK OR TREAT

Even before they were teenagers, the generation born 1925–1942 caught the attention of their elders with the Halloween slogan "trick or treat." True, they weren't the first generation to commemorate Halloween by calling on neighbors and begging for treats, nor by disrupting neighborhoods with pranks ranging from smashing pumpkins to absconding with anything portable. But it was the generation later to be called Silent, perhaps with the aid of their parents, who came up with the idea of offering householders a choice of chaos or candy by saying "trick or treat."

Many new words are such obvious derivations of older ones that they were invented independently more than once. For example, one source says *bobbysoxer* was invented by Sinatra's publicist George Evans. He probably did invent it, but most likely others had too. It was a natural extension of "bobby sox."

But *trick or treat* is distinctive enough that it probably had a unique inventor. Most likely it was someone from the west of the United States or Canada. That's because the earliest evidence we have so far is from the western parts of those countries. As far back as 1927 a newspaper in Lethbridge in southern Alberta,

Canada, not far from the border with Montana, reported from the little town of Blackie:

> *"Trick or Treat" Is Demand.*
>
> *No real damage was done except to the temper of some who had to hunt for wagon wheels, gates, wagons, barrels, etc., much of which decorated the front street. The youthful tormentors were at back door and front demanding edible plunder by the word "trick or treat" to which the inmates gladly responded and sent the robbers away rejoicing.*

Similar early newspaper citations of "trick or treat" come from the United States: Portland, Oregon, in 1934; Porter County, Indiana, in 1937; Reno, Nevada, and Helena, Montana, in 1938; Centralia, Washington, in 1939.

What had they been saying before "trick or treat"? Well, "Shell out!" was one demand, dating back at least to the early 19th century in conversation. That was what one observer heard across the border in Toronto at Halloween 1941. But "trick or treat" had the advantage of being more polite, more poetic, and more politic.

By the 1940s, "trick or treat" had gone nationwide, as evidenced by a poem with that title in the November 1, 1941, issue of the *Saturday Evening Post*. It begins:

> *Pumpkin moon*
> *In a witch-black sky,*
> *And—was that a bat wing*
> *Rustling by?*

And ringing your bell,
    An awesome band—
Ghost and goblin,
    Hand in hand,
Spook and scarecrow and painted clown,
    Shrilling, "Trick or treat!" from pint-size down.

Better be ready!
    Better beware!
Better not find your larder bare
    Of candy apples and hickory nuts
And gingerbread in generous cuts
    And walnut-coconut-cream delights.
Ghosts have remarkable
    Appetites!
Treat them to popcorn
    In a poke,
And they'll play their tricks
    On meaner folk!

A 1941 issue of *Gleanings in Bee Culture* offered help to homeowners: "Just in case you live in a town where 'trick or treat' rule holds sway on that night, I have included some toothsome recipes for some honey goodies that you can hand out to these would-be pranksters."

Popular Science magazine, in a 1942 article "How to Tell a Movie Story with a Series of Still Photographs," suggests "With limitless subject matter right at your elbow, you should have little difficulty in picking an idea.... the children threatening trick-or-treat on Halloween—these are all ideas."

And Brach's candies declared in their 1942 annual report: "As one of the three biggest candy occasions of the year, Halloween found Brach's ready with a full line for the Trick or Treat set."

A contributor to *American Notes & Queries* in 1942 explained: "Youngsters here [upstate Illinois] have adopted what appears to be a new set of tactics. They rang the doorbell a night or so before Halloween, last year, to deliver their 'Trick or treat' ultimatum—and to size up the prospects! On the 'real' Halloween they returned, well costumed and masked (and noticeably polite). They just wanted to 'show themselves,' they said. I treated them and they left quickly."

Little has changed in Halloween customs since "trick or treat" became the watchword of the Silents, except that rumors of poison or worse in homemade treats have outlawed them in most places, in favor of store-bought goodies.

THE BOOM GENERATION

(born 1943–1960)

Many generations have competing names, with advocates for each designation arguing which label is most salient. But there's no alternative name for the generation known as Baby Boomers or Boomers. Their name is firmly tied to a statistic, the growing number of babies born in the years after World War II.

Strangely, there was a brief prewar baby boom too, as *Life* magazine noted on December 1, 1941, in the final days of peace for the United States before the December 7 Pearl Harbor attack. "Adolf Hitler has proclaimed that this world war is an inevitable struggle between his fertile German Reich and such sterile old nations as the U.S. and Great Britain," *Life* declared. "But this year a great baby boom has pushed the U.S. birth rate up to 18.5 babies per thousand of population, while Nazi Germany is declining from its 1939 high of 20.5. If the trend goes on, next year may see the U.S. winning the baby war against Hitler, in birth rate as well as total production." But this was nothing compared to what would come after the war.

According to the U.S. Census, the midcentury increase in births that gave rise to the term "baby boom" was a postwar phenomenon. Where there had been 2.8 million births in the United States in 1945, there were 3.5 million in 1946, and the number increased every year to 4.3 million in 1961. The annual totals then went slightly down to 4 million in 1964 and steeply downward after that. The birth rate per thousand women went from 20.4 in 1945 to a peak of 25.3 in 1954 and remained above 20 until 1965. From that date to this the rate has never reached 20 again; in 2009 it was only 13.8. Demographically, then, the years of the baby boom are 1946 to 1964, when a total of nearly 80 million Americans were born.

Despite these facts, Strauss and Howe argue for different starting and ending dates for the Boomers, based not on birth rates but on the mindset of the postwar era. Those born 1943 and later, they note, have no memory of World War II, and for those born 1961 and later, World War II had receded as a determining factor. "Their eighteen years of birth began [in 1943] with the first real evidence that G.I. optimism would be rewarded with victory and ended [in 1960] with the first election of a G.I. President," they explain.

Whether the Boomers' birth years are 1946–1961 or 1943–1964, in any case, the distinctive behavior of the Boomers remains essentially the same. And by their distinctive actions and words, Baby Boomers brought the whole notion of generations to the fore.

What made them distinctive? Strauss and Howe, calling Boomers an "idealist" generation, summed them up as self-absorbed and smug, sure of themselves and of their ways, and endlessly reinventing themselves from hippie to yuppie to present-day helicopter parents.

TOOTH FAIRY

Early in life, baby Baby Boomers cut their teeth on the life of privilege by spreading the word on the Tooth Fairy. Baby teeth start coming out around age six, when the distinction between the world of magic and the world of reality is still not so clear. And the loss of the first baby tooth is a big event for a child that age. It's not known who came up with the idea of exchanging a tooth under the pillow for cash, but once someone did, the word got around, perhaps more via the six–year-old grapevine than the adult.

One of the earliest published stories about the Tooth Fairy illustrates this. Lee Rogow, in a story simply titled "The Tooth Fairy" in *Collier's* for August 20, 1949, tells of little Cynthia, age five years, three months, and two days, who loses her first tooth. Cynthia explains to her parents, "If you put your tooth under your pillow at night, the tooth fairy comes and leaves ten cents. Susan Bowen got ten cents yesterday." Her modern, scientific parents try to disabuse Cynthia of the notion of a tooth fairy, but in vain. "Maybe it's something grownups don't know about," Cynthia says. And though the parents tell each other that it will be good for Cynthia to learn that there's no tooth fairy, each of them privately puts a dime under Cynthia's pillow, so in the morning Cynthia exclaims, "Two dimes. Oh, wait till I see that dopey Sandra Bowen!"

It's possible that the idea of a tooth fairy came from Esther Watkins Arnold, who wrote a three-act play for children called "The Tooth Fairy," published as long ago as 1927. But it was around 1950 that the practice of the tooth fairy exchanging teeth for money under the pillow became widespread. Child-to-child comparisons of the amounts the tooth fairy left, as in Cynthia's story, may have been the greatest motivation for increasing the award to a present-day average of $3, according to a 2012 survey.

TEENYBOPPER

Teenager, that label first applied en masse to the Silent Generation, was such a resonant concept that it spawned two terms first applied en masse to the Boomers. One was *teenybopper*, so called with reference to music designed to appeal to young teen girls. Anne Hollander called it "sugary teenybopper pop" in her 1968 *Sunday's Child: Love, Loss & Redemption in a Texas Wine Bar.* In *Portnoy's Complaint*, Arnold says to his companion, a woman he calls The

Monkey, "Almost three days, and I haven't heard the hillbilly routine, the Betty-Boop-dumb-cunt routine, the *teenybopper* bit."

"How does the reference librarian manage the new generation of teenyboppers?" asked *RQ*, journal of the Reference Services Division of the American Library Association in 1965. "Is the teenybopper a definite threat to the traditional concept of service to young adults?"

HIPPIE

And then the 1960s came along, and the cute little boys and girls and the teenyboppers, offspring of G.I. parents, in large numbers turned their backs on their elders and created their own new world, quite different from the teen culture of the Silents who had gone before them.

The '60s saw civil rights marches and legislation ending segregation in the South, an escalating war in Vietnam and growing numbers of Boomers drafted for it, new drugs like LSD leading to new adventures of the mind, and the Pill for contraception available for the first time, leading to a sexual revolution.

And how did the Boomers react? They inherited rock and roll and turned it into revolution. They protested segregation and the war. In Timothy Leary's famous phrase, they turned on, tuned in, and dropped out—at least many of them did. And the result was the hippie.

The Silents had had a few counter-culture rebels of their own, known as *hipsters* and *beatniks*. You could find them in Greenwich Village or at City Lights Books in San Francisco, Beat poets like Allen Ginsberg (born 1926) with his 1955 *Howl*:

> I saw the best minds of my generation destroyed by madness, starving
>   hysterical naked,
> dragging themselves through the negro streets at dawn looking for an
>   angry fix,
> angelheaded hipsters burning for the ancient heavenly connection to
>   the starry dynamo in the machinery of night,
> who poverty and tatters and hollow-eyed and high sat up smoking in
>   the supernatural darkness of cold-water flats floating across the
>   tops of cities contemplating jazz,. . .

But in the culture of the '60s, the few hipsters of the previous generation were displaced by the numerous Boomer *hippies*. By no means was every Boomer a hippie, but the appeal and influence of the hippies were widespread.

Hippies were mellow rather than mad, sometimes naked but not starving or hysterical, and high mainly on pot. A professor at the University of Michigan in 1967 saw their defining characteristics as being an emphasis on individuality; unconventionality of dress; peace, not war; and use of drugs, especially marijuana. And of course they had hair, long long hair.

To say hippies called attention to themselves is an understatement. A short-lived magazine at Berkeley in 1965 took its name

SPIDER as an acronym for its provocative themes: Sex, Politics, International communism, Drugs, Extremism, and Rock and roll. That quickly succeeded in getting it banned from being sold on campus.

Naturally, there was a flood of books to explore the hippie phenomenon. They included, in 1967:

- *Confessions of a Part-time Hippie* by Laura W.
- *Hippie Morality, More Old than New*
- *Household Hints for Hippie Housewives*
- *Hippie Is Necessary to Explore What the Old Denies and the New Predicts*

And in 1968:

- *Teen Hippie*
- *The Hippie Papers: Notes from the Underground Press*
- *Sex-Happy Hippie*

as well as "101 Hippie Jokes" by Paul Laikin for *Sick* magazine. Jokes like these:

- *What's green, blue, red, purple, lavender, chartreuse and lilac?*
- *A well-dressed hippie.*
- *To a hippie, what is police brutality?*
- *Getting slapped by a cop while trying to kiss him.*

- *What is the plural of hippie?*
- *Love-in.*
- *Why do girl hippies wear yellow slacks?*
- *To tell them apart from the boy hippies.*

The hippie phenomenon was short-lived but influential. After at most a decade, hippie Boomers put their tie-dyes in the back of their closets and moved into more conventional satisfied self-centered adulthood. But the influence of hippiedom persisted. The variety of present-day American culture in clothing, food, language, and music, to name just a few areas, had its beginning in the hippie reaction to the monoculture of their day.

Nowadays someone who wants to be a hippie needs the help of *The Hippie Handbook: How to Tie-Dye a T-Shirt, Flash a Peace Sign, and Other Essential Skills for the Carefree Life*, published in 2004 by Chelsea Cain, who grew up on a hippie commune in Iowa. She writes:

> *There was a time when hippies did not need jobs and frolicked freely in the Haight-Ashbury and in soy fields throughout the fertile Midwest. These times are over.*
>
> *Between 1965 and 1975, hippies figured out how to do a lot of stuff....We made candles and clothes and hanging plant holders, not because these things weren't available elsewhere but because not buying stuff was a radical act of social resistance.*

Hippies, she explains, "represent all that is optimistic and outrageous and youthful in each of us. Plus, they have the best hair."

LOVE-IN AND BE-IN

The 1960s were marked by political activism too. Serious Silents took part in sit-ins at lunch counters in the Southern states, blacks and whites sitting side by side to end the whites-only policy. Later in that decade student activists took the sit-in strategy back to their campuses in the North and West for their own protests against college administrations and the Vietnam War. They held teach-ins to raise political awareness.

Less serious Boomers in California had a flowering of counterculture in the mid-1960s, culminating in the "summer of love" in 1967 that also disseminated short-lived new vocabulary for the groovy "flower people": "-in" words based on the model of *sit-in* and *teach-in*.

At the Monterey Pop Festival that summer, Scott McKenzie sang, "If you're going to San Francisco, be sure to wear some flowers in your hair." Why? Because "you're going to meet some gentle people there," and indeed, young hippies from all over the country did just that. "There's a whole generation with a new explanation," McKenzie continued, and "If you come to San Francisco, summertime will be a love-in there."

Earlier that year, in mid-January, at Golden Gate Park in San Francisco, some 20,000 hippies and activists came together for a political rally and music festival to protest a new state law banning LSD. The occasion, featuring Allen Ginsberg, Timothy Leary, the Grateful Dead, Jefferson Airplane, and many others, was announced as "A gathering of the tribes for a Human Be-In."

Be-In was a singular word for a singular event, but *love-in* has survived beyond the hippie era.

FLOWER POWER AND FLOWER CHILDREN

With a little help from their friends in the Silent Generation, hippies during the 1960s celebrated *flower power*. The initial impetus for the phrase came from a 1965 essay by beat poet Allen Ginsberg suggesting that nonviolent demonstrators face hostile adversaries with "masses of flowers—a visual spectacle—especially concentrated in the front lines." The media quickly generated the rhyming pair *flower power* and the derivatives *flower people* and *flower children* for those who came to San Francisco for the summer of love with flowers in their hair. Fragile and utopian as it was, flower power managed to inspire for a few years, until the end of the 1960s.

GROOVY

For a while in the 1960s and 1970s, as they were growing up, Boomers were *groovy*. They outgrew groovy later, but if there was a word that characterized the '60s and '70s lifestyle, it was *groovy*.

Google Ngrams and the Corpus of Historical American English show that it shot up in popularity in the mid-1960s and peaked in the early 1970s, dropping down again as that decade came to an end.

Before the Boomers came along, *groovy* had been around for decades as a jazz term, derived from and meaning the same as "in the groove." It's in Ralph Ellison's *Invisible Man*, published 1952, where the bartender Barrelhouse asks, "You like the groovy music on the juke?"

What *groovy* meant when Boomers adopted it in the mid-sixties was more than merely cool. It was a whole new way of life, epitomized in 1966 in Paul Simon and Art Garfunkel's "59th Street Bridge Song" that popularized the word:

Slow down, you move too fast, you've got to make the morning last
Just kickin' down the cobble-stones, lookin' for fun and feelin' groovy
Feeling groovy
Hello lamp-post, what cha knowin', I've come to watch your flowers growin'
Ain't cha got no rhymes for me, do-it-do-do, feelin' groovy
Feeling groovy
I've got no deeds to do, no promises to keep
I'm dappled and drowsy and ready to sleep
Let the morning time drop all its petals on me
Life I love you, all is groovy

"The happiest song on earth," someone has said on YouTube.

What's groovy? In 1967, *The New Yorker's* "Talk of the Town" interviewed a twenty-three-year-old, Diana Dew, a designer of "electronic clothes," who was fully into the new hippie lifestyle. At the University of Florida several years earlier, she explained, "I started turning on. You know, making the acid scene off campus—LSD, peyote, all the hallucinogens—with the hipper students and professors. Turning on got me back in the whole creative bag." She converted a Volkswagen bus into a camper and headed west. "It was real groovy," she said. "I took my time. Camping out under the stars. I needed to he alone.—I was still trying to figure out who I was."

Another glimpse of the groovy lifestyle came when a reporter for *New York* magazine in 1969 called about an ad in the *Village Voice* for "Shares available in groovy, coed house" on Fire Island, Davis Park. "We really have a groovy group, ya know?" said the woman who answered the phone. "But *friendly* groovy, ya know? One guy wanted to know if 'groovy' meant we held whipped-cream parties." They did not.

Perhaps the ultimate *groovy* comes in Joan Didion's 1968 collection of essays, *Slouching Toward Bethlehem: Life Styles in the Golden Land*:

> *It is a pretty nice day and I am just driving down the*
> *Street and I see Barbara at a light.*
> *What am I doing, she wants to know.*
> *I am just driving around.*
> *"Groovy," she says.*

It's a beautiful day, I say.
"Groovy," she agrees.
She wants to know if I will come over. Sometime
soon, I say.
"Groovy," she says.

TRIP AND PSYCHEDELIC

When hippies traveled, the trips were often in their minds. Powered by psychedelics, notably the recently synthesized LSD, they explored the far reaches of consciousness. And like travelers of the conventional kind, they had guides and guidebooks for their trips, to make sure they would have a good experience and to let them know what to expect.

The most prominent guide and advocate for "acid trips" was psychologist Timothy Leary, a researcher and lecturer at Harvard. He promoted the psychedelic experience enthusiastically and was coauthor of the first guidebook for LSD trips, *The Psychedelic Experience: A Manual Based on The Tibetan Book of the Dead* (1964). In 1966 he made a recording of substantial parts of the book, to serve as an audio guide for someone taking an acid trip. In a calm encouraging voice, Leary details each step as the traveler goes out from everyday consciousness, visits unknown places, and comes back to the world as we know it, enlightened.

Leary's charismatic proselytizing for LSD got him dismissed from Harvard in 1963, but he continued undaunted to promote trips with the slogan he first proclaimed at the 1967 Human Be-In in San Francisco: "Turn on, tune in, drop out."

Psychedelic was coined in the late 1950s by Humphry Osmond, a psychiatrist who knew his Greek, combining *psyche* meaning "mind" with *del* meaning "reveal." Osmond was born in 1917 and Leary in 1920, long before the Boomer generation. But it was the young Boomers who experimented most enthusiastically with psychedelic trips. "I get high with a little help from my friends," sang the Beatles in 1967.

And trips weren't limited to LSD or marijuana. *Newsweek* in 1967 reported, "Now the claim that banana skins are the newest ticket to a psychedelic trip has touched off a banana-buying boom from the Haight-Asbury district to Harvard Square."

FUCK

As Boomers grew older, most of them left hippiedom behind, taking conventional jobs, dressing conventionally, leaving bell-bottom pants and tie-dyed shirts in the back of closets for their children to wonder about. Hippie language too became dated, especially *groovy* as a synonym for *cool*.

But they had instigated a major change in the English language, bringing *fuck* and other four-letter words out of the closet.

By no means was *fuck* a new word. The *Oxford English Dictionary* shows examples from as far back as 1568, and says the word is likely to be older but unattested because it has been "one of the

English words most avoided as taboo." Dictionaries avoided it, even the biggest and most comprehensive like the *Oxford English Dictionary* itself (before 1972) and the "Unabridged," Webster's *New International Dictionary* of 1961 that shocked reviewers for its supposed permissiveness. *Fuck* was used plentifully enough where dictionaries feared to tread, in men-only conversations and particularly in the military. The World War II military acronyms SNAFU and FUBAR, explained euphemistically as "situation normal, all fouled up" and "fouled up beyond all recognition," are evidence of that earlier taboo use. Women for the most part avoided it altogether.

All that changed beginning in the 1960s, thanks to the Boomers. Nowadays *fuck* is heard and seen in many contexts, freely used by women as well as men, often in movies and novels, and with concomitant lessening of its shock value. Nowadays a *clusterfuck* is just a term for everything going wrong, and *Bumfuck* is a well-known nickname for a small town in the middle of nowhere. A style of high-heeled women's shoes is now known as *fuck-me pumps,* with help from a 2003 song of that name by Amy Winehouse. The term is so familiar that it inspired a cartoon in *The New Yorker* of a woman saying to a shoe store sales clerk, "I need a really great pair of marry-me pumps." There are also *CFMBs, come fuck me boots.*

Exactly when and how did this seismic shift in the English language take place? In this case, I think it's possible to pinpoint the flap of the butterfly wings that rippled out to cause such a storm of change.

The time was the morning of March 3, 1965. The epicenter, the place from which the change spread, was in Berkeley, California, at Telegraph and Bancroft Avenues, the southern entrance to the University of California campus. And it all began with a sheet of paper on which a young man had written the word *fuck*.

All eyes were on Berkeley at that time, filled with Boomer undergraduates, because of the student-led Free Speech Movement that had resulted in victory for student activists the year before. With nonviolent sit-ins and marches, during the fall semester 1964 they had persuaded the university to lift its ban on political advocacy at the edge of campus. Just as the F.S.M. had spontaneously attracted wide support from students, so it spontaneously disbanded when its work was done.

What does this have to do with language and generations? The lofty and virtuous F.S.M. was the background for a decidedly unlofty protest during the relative calm of the semester that followed.

John Thompson, a drifter and would-be poet, best characterized as a "slacker" before Generation X reinvented the term, on that morning in March was sitting on a planter at the edge of the main entrance to campus. Just to get a little attention, hoping even to enhance his reputation by getting thrown in jail, he wrote FUCK on a piece of notebook paper and held it up.

Nothing happened at first, but after a while a "frat guy" came up, angrily took the paper and tore it up. After he left, Thompson calmly wrote another, more elaborate and academic sign: "FUCK (verb)." And after another while the frat guy came back with a policeman, who arrested him.

And thus a new cause was born. It was soon labeled another F.S.M., the "Filthy Speech Movement," much to the delight of the hippie Boomers, much to the disgust of certain high-minded civil rights and antiwar activists, the responsible members of the Silent Generation.

Holding up the sign was a Boomer thing to do. Thompson, born in 1942, was one year too old for Boomerdom, but younger Boomers began to follow his lead. Not by holding up signs with four-letter words, but by casually using them, nice middle-class boys and girls who up till then would not have filled their mouths with words like "fuck." With his sign, Thompson had found another way to shock the establishment. Abbie Hoffman summed it up in the title of his 1967 book, *Fuck the System*.

Over the course of a decade or so, the shock waves spread so widely that they no longer shocked, and "fuck" became merely an edgy word rather than a shockingly taboo one. Authors like Hoffman discovered that they could get attention by using the word. So did Michael McCloskey in his 1968 volume of short stories simply titled, *Fuck You*.

The generational effect is evident in the dialogue from a 1969 collection of short stories, *Nightwork* by Christine Schutt. "What are you writing?" a mother asks her daughter. "Fuck fuck fuck fuck fuck for pages," says the daughter, who "seemed happy to say it, *fuck*."

Erica Jong made a name for herself with her 1973 novel, *Fear of Flying*, notable for her coinage of the term *zipless fuck*, "absolutely pure" and "free of ulterior motives," where "zippers fall away like rose petals."

The spreading use of *fuck* is a dramatic moment in a 1980 book *Voyeur Wife* by Nick Eastwood. Cheryl, a suburban wife, spies on her sister Amy as she says to her husband, "are you going to go on teasing me, darling, or are we going to fuck?" The book continues:

> *Cheryl stifled a shocked gasp. She hadn't known that her stylish, rich older sister used words like that. Their upbringing had been very strict, and Cheryl personally did not approve of dirty language.*
>
> *Where had Amy learned such filthy words? . . . this was not the prim college girl that Cheryl remembered. Her sister was behaving like a common slut.*

Responding to the trend, both for shock value but also because of gradual acceptance, movies began using *fuck* in the 1970s. The intensity peaked in the 1980s. Those who bother to keep score found 208 *fucks* in *Scarface* (1983), 159 in *Platoon* (1986), and 157 in *Colors* (1988).

Dictionaries began including the word in the 1970s, with the realization that people would be more likely to buy dictionaries than to banish them if they included it. The *American Heritage Dictionary* of 1969 was one of the first. Even the famously prudish *New Yorker* finally accepted *fuck* on its pages beginning in 1985.

STREAKING

As hippies, Boomers managed to shock their elders with their uncensored use of language and their unconventional clothing. They managed to shock without clothing too. In a last gasp for Boomers before handing over young adulthood to Generation X, college students across the country went *streaking* in 1973 and 1974.

Places where large numbers of students congregated were especially likely targets—auditoriums, cafeterias, and in good weather out of doors near student residences. Bursting into view stark naked before a usually appreciative audience, students would rush past and quickly disappear. That speed inspired the name for the activity, coined by a reporter in Washington, D.C., who called in a story from a phone booth, saying that hundreds of naked students at the University of Maryland were "streaking past."

At Northwestern University near Chicago, television news on March 19, 1974, included an interview with a student who had been attending an English class: "Well, we were listening to a lecture on Madame Bovary, when all of a sudden a guy comes in, streaking right down the aisle, then around up on the stage, dancing around, and then he left—streaking. It was really great."

There was streaking in the streets at night. "It's amazing," said another eyewitness. "I haven't seen so many Northwestern students around since I've been here. All of a sudden you see thousands of students around. It's really exciting."

They interviewed a streaker who explained, "Just wanted to try and see what it was like. I jog at night, so it was a good way to try it."

In downstate Jacksonville, Illinois, one spring night the two local colleges had a "streak-off" along the road that connected them. Students from both colleges applauded as streakers streaked by.

Streaking had happened before 1973 and continued after 1974, but 1974 was the golden moment.

LIFESTYLE

Around 1970, as Boomers began to move beyond hippiedom to young adulthood, their expanding choices gave them a new perspective on life and a new word to describe it: *lifestyle*. At first it was two words, *life style*, but soon the two words became the one-word name for the opportunity to choose how to live.

Nowadays, as we continue to enjoy a variety of lifestyles, it's hard to picture how limited Americans had been in their daily lives before the 1960s. It wasn't because of any government edict that people tended to dress alike, eat alike, travel alike, entertain themselves alike; it was more of an unconscious consensus encouraged by the mass media.

Before the sixties, women raised or lowered the hemlines of their skirts every year according to styles introduced by designers, even if they owned no designer clothes. Going downtown in a city, or attending church or a play, meant dresses for women and coats and ties for men. Before the sixties, home-cooked meals were generally guided by *The Joy of Cooking*. One kind of coffee was available. Cars were made in Detroit by the "Big Three." Television was available on three networks and just a handful of other channels. There was one kind of American beer, available from a handful of big breweries. Intoxication came from alcohol, not drugs. Colleges imposed curfews on women students. Even telephones were alike, and you would have to pay extra for any color other than black. And there were words you'd never say in polite company, much less allow in a dictionary in your house.

But the sixties changed that. Hippies dressed in flamboyant outfits, the polar opposite of convention, and suddenly anything else up to that extreme was possible. Women could wear skirts as short or as long as they wished, and they could wear pants anytime. And what went for clothing went for everything else. You could choose your own lifestyle. There were books to help, of course, like *Toward a Self-Managed Life Style* (1975).

Different kinds of relationships were possible too. A review of Frieda Porat and Karen Myers's *Changing Your Life Style* (1973) sums it up: there are "new options now available thanks to the impact of the pill, the vasectomy, Women's Lib, encounter groups and hippie communes.... The New Man needs help in getting in touch with his emotions; the Liberated Woman needs to rid herself of the assumption that her identity is defined by her relationship to a man. Everyone needs greater self-esteem." This of course could lead to *Open Marriage: A New Life Style for Couples* (1975).

SELF-ESTEEM

Self-esteem wasn't a new term when the Boomers were young. It predated them by three centuries. But it was the Boomers who picked up on the importance of self-esteem, and they were proud to have it. This was reflected in book titles of the time: *Enhancing Student Self-Esteem* (1967) and *Your Child's Self Esteem: The Key to Life* (1975).

YUPPIE

As the 1960s faded into history, so did the Boomer hippies. What happened to them? Linguistically they receded for a decade, to emerge in 1982 transformed in both lifestyle and language as *yuppies*—taking an acronym for Young Urban Professionals as the first syllable, while keeping the second as a tribute to their hippie past.

A 1982 article in *Commentary* was among the first mentions of the new word, describing yuppies as "those people who are undecided about growing up; they are college-educated, getting on and even getting up in the world, but with a bit of the hippie-dippie counterculture clinging to them still." By 1984 *yuppie* was well enough known to bring forth a best seller, *The Yuppie*

Handbook: The State-of-the-Art Manual for Young Urban Professionals. Authors Marissa Piesman and Marilee Hartley gave this definition of their subject:

> *A person of either sex who meets the following criteria: 1) resides in or near one of the major cities; 2) claims to be between the ages of 25 and 45; 3) lives on aspirations of glory, prestige, recognition, fame, social status, power, money or any and all combinations of the above; 4) anyone who brunches on the weekend or works out after work. The term crosses ethnic, sexual, geographic—even class—boundaries. Adj.: Yuppiesque, Yuppie-like, Yuppish.*

But Boomers had their choice of lifestyles, so *hippie* morphed not only into *yuppie* but into variations on the theme:

BUPPIE: black urban professional.
HUPPIE: Hispanic urban professional.
PUPPIE: poor urban professional.
DINKIE: dual income, no kids.

Not every Boomer was a yuppie, of course. Strauss and Howe point out that "Only some 5 percent of the Boom match the demographic (urban, professional, affluent) definition" of *yuppie*. But a "much larger proportion fit the subjective definition: self-immersion, an impatient desire for personal satisfaction, and weak civic instincts."

GAY

Perhaps the biggest turnaround in the English language during the 20th century was the happy little word *gay*. For more than six hundred years this word kept the core meaning it had when it was borrowed from Norman French in the Middle Ages: brilliant, light-hearted, cheerful. The brevity of the word went well with the lightness of its meaning.

It wasn't so long ago that *gay* held that original meaning, without irony. Here are a few examples from that bygone era. There's the children's rhyme:

Over in the meadow,
Where the grass is so even,
Lived a gay mother cricket
And her little crickets seven.
"Chirp!" said the mother;
"We chirp!" said the seven,
So they chirped cheery notes,
In the grass soft and even.

From *Skyscraper*, a 1931 novel by Faith Baldwin:

> *They went out on the terrace together, and together leaned over the parapet and looked out over the lower city. The terrace was gay with the hardiest of spring*

flowers, with small, squat trees in green pottery jars,
with chairs of decorative metal, swinging couches, tables.
    She drew a deep breath of pleasure and astonishment.
"How very lovely!" she told him, entranced.
    "I like it. Later, we have gay awnings and parasols.
All it then lacks is sand and sea," he told her laughing.

From an ad for Ten High 80 proof whiskey in *Life* magazine for December 18, 1939: "To say 'Merry Christmas'—say 'Ten High.' And give it in this gay, gifty carton that says, 'I want to double your enjoyment of the holidays!' "

From Lillian Hellman's 1952 play *The Autumn Garden*: Rose says, "Well, I feel young and gay, and I'm going to a party." Much later, Ned Crossman says: "You came here a nice little girl who had seen war and trouble. You had spirit in a quiet way, and you were gay, in a quiet way, which is the only way women should be gay, since they are never really gay at all. Only serious people are ever gay."

From *The Latin Language* by Leonard Robert Palmer (1954): "Our linguistic gesturings and posings assume adaptations appropriate to the given occasion, formal, grave, and stiff in conference, informal, gay, and relaxed in the company of our intimates."

From a four-page brochure for a Georgian Bay Line excursion boat: "Join this Gay Tulip-time Cherryland Weekend Cruise from Chicago to Holland, Michigan and Sturgeon Bay, Wisconsin, May 17–20, 1957."

And from *Gay Monarch: The Life and Pleasures of Edward VII* (1956) by Virginia Cowles. As a boy, Edward paid "a state visit to the gay imperial court of Napoleon III and the beautiful Empress Eugenie."

No hint of homosexuality in any of those, in fact no hint of sex. But the *Oxford English Dictionary* shows that the original *gay* can mean "dedicated to social pleasures; dissolute, promiscuous; frivolous, hedonistic. Also (esp. in *to go gay*): uninhibited; wild, crazy; flamboyant." And the *Oxford English Dictionary* gives "Gay nineties" as an example, a nickname for the 1890s invented a few decades later.

Toward the end of the 20th century, as homosexuals began affirming their orientation more and more openly, *gay* became attached to that lifestyle. At first it seemed too frivolous for serious discussion, but *gay* has managed to become the preferred designation, particularly for men. Even the most serious publications and conversations about male homosexuals now use *gay* as the standard term.

And the change in attitude leading to wide acceptance of the gay lifestyle and the use of *gay* for it in the 21st century had its beginning with the Boomers.

MS.

No, the first feminists weren't Boomers. But the Boomer generation was the first generation to have substantial numbers of feminists. And they adopted a new title to reflect their new attitude and lifestyle: *Ms.*

It's difficult to change a basic element of language. Years of attempts to substitute a gender-neutral singular pronoun to replace *she* and *he* have failed. But Boomers did succeed in gaining acceptance for that marriage-neutral title for women. It wasn't brand new, but it remained on the fringe of English until Gloria Steinem brought it to prominence as the title of her magazine *Ms.*, which started in 1972. Steinem, born 1934, was an unsilent member of the Silent Generation, but the Boomers were the ones who especially heeded her call. After all, they believed in freedom.

In a 2012 interview with Marlo Thomas, Steinem recalled: "We chose *Ms.* because it was not only symbolic, but short and took up less cover space. We actually found that word in secretarial handbooks of the 1950s, as a way of dealing with the embarrassment of not knowing whether a woman was married or not. But later, we discovered it was on a tombstone from the 1700s; and in England, it had been in use for centuries as an abbreviation for 'Mistress.' Since even children were called Master and Mistress, it meant female without marital status."

SINGLE PARENT

In the mid-20th century, unmarried women who had committed the act of having a child were generally known as *unmarried women* or *unwed mothers.* And those were not terms of endearment. "Unwed motherhood . . . leads to shame, disgrace, physical discomfort, and pain," wrote Gertrude Florence Barker in a 1967 dissertation.

In barely more than a decade, both of those terms were in decline, and a new less stigmatized designation, *single parent*, became the norm.

Google Ngrams show that in the 1960s, *unwed mother* was twice as likely to appear in print as *single parent,* and *unmarried mother* four times as likely. By 1975, however, *single parent* appears more often than either of the others, and by 1980 *single parent* was seven times more prevalent than either. It far exceeded *divorcee* too.

Books published in the late 20th century increasingly reflected the positive connotations of *single parent: The Single Parent and Her Baby: Implications for Community Action* (1967), *Everything a Single Parent Needs to Know* (1976), *Sex and the Single Parent: How You Can Have Happy and Healthy Kids—and an Active Social Life* (1986), *The Single-Parent Family: Living Happily in a Changing Word* (1994).

Single parents were generally women, but it was recognized that men could be single parents too. That deliberate ambiguity helped lift the opprobrium on women. "I remember the relief in that label versus the alternatives when my son was due on my 20th birthday in 1980!" commented a woman on the AllExperts website. Since then the term *single mother*, a rarity until the 1980s, in the early 21st century has become as dominant as *single parent.*

The great increase in *single parent* and *single mother* have gone along with a great increase in the number of single parents and single mothers. In 1960, 9 percent of children lived with a single parent. That percentage had tripled by the time of the 2010 census. Mothers remain predominant; four-fifths of unmarried parents are women.

BLENDED FAMILY

Yet another lifestyle that became prevalent among Boomers first was the *blended family*. The term first appears around 1970 and became prominent around 1990, as increasing numbers of Boomers divorced and remarried and brought their children with them into their combined household. Books on the topic proliferated in the 1980s: *I Married a Family: Step-parenting and the Blended Family* (1981), *The Stepfather and the Blended Family* (1982), *The Blended Family* (1984) by Tom and Adrienne Frydenger: "When you marry and form a nuclear family, you usually have one set of in-laws and one set of children. Marrying into a blended family, however, is like jumping head first into chaos."

By the 1990s the books became more positive: *Love in the Blended Family* (1991), *Growing as a Blended Family* (1994), *Coping in a Blended Family* (1997), *Positive Discipline in Blended Families: Nurturing Harmony* (1997), *Surviving and Thriving as a Blended Family* (1999).

The Brady Bunch, the 1969–1974 television sitcom, even more popular now in reruns, was the model, or perhaps the ideal, for a blended family. With divorce proliferating, remarriages and blended families became almost the norm. According to the website WinningStepfamilies, nowadays one of three Americans is involved in a blended relationship and "more than half of Americans today have been, are now or will eventually be in one or more step situations during their lives."

FAST FOOD AND JUNK FOOD

Yes, Boomers introduced *fast food* and *junk food* too. One Boomer lifestyle centered on Happy Meals, another shunned the junk in favor of locally grown organics. *Fast food* took off in the 1960s, *junk food* a decade later in response, though that scolding term has never caught up with *fast food* in popularity.

The campaign against junk food was in high gear in 1978, with the publication of books like *The Teenager's Concept of Junk Food, The Junk Food Withdrawal Manual, Kick the Junk Food Habit with Snackers*, as well as the slightly more positive *The Junk Food Junkie's Haute Cuisine*. There was even *The Junk Food Blues: Starring M.T. Calorie, with Nutricia and Doc!* a thirty-two-page booklet published that year by the March of Dimes.

A specific example of the response to junk food comes in Eleanor Levitt's *Natural Food Cookery* (1979): "Since most of today's packaged candy, crackers, sugar-coated cereals and soft drinks are 'junk' food, I substitute raw, unsalted nuts and an array of tasty seeds, fresh fruit, unsalted popcorn and raisins, for the commercial treats."

HELICOPTER PARENT

Throughout their lives, Boomers have known what they wanted. And they have known what they want for their children, too, who generally belong to the Millennials. When little, their children are watched, scheduled, and protected from all possible dangers. At college, children of such parents communicate daily with parents and get help dealing with administrators, professors, and fellow students. In this phase of their assertiveness, Boomer parents have been called *helicopter parents* since at least 1989.

In 2003, *Psychology Today* noted, "With such a high level of emotional and financial investment, many parents see the status of their adult children as a final parental exam. And parents don't want a bad grade—either for themselves or for their kids. Not surprisingly, parental involvement in kids' lives has pushed its way onto campuses, where 'helicopter parents' hover."

It's not a complimentary term, and it's used mainly by pundits, psychologists, and dispensers of advice on child-raising, who self-righteously condemn the practice. Not that Boomers are likely to listen.

DECIDER

"I hear the voices, and I read the front page, and I know the speculation," said President George W. Bush on April 18, 2006. "But

I'm the decider, and I decide what is best. And what's best is for Don Rumsfeld to remain as the Secretary of Defense."

Bush, born in 1946, is a Boomer. His use of *decider* prompted parodies, T shirts, and a comic book on the Daily Show featuring Bush as a caped superhero, The Decider. He hadn't been heard using *decider* earlier in his life, and he didn't put it to everyday use after that occasion. Nor did other Boomers adopt it. Nevertheless, Bush's linguistic creativity provided a word that aptly characterizes the Boomer attitude.

AWESOME

Awesome is a word not particularly limited to Boomers, although it has appeared with increasing frequency during the Boomers' progression from birth to senior citizenship. But it's a word that some Boomers, at least, apply to themselves. There's a website called "The Boomer Blogs: A Place for That Awesome Generation, Boomers!" and another called "The Awesome Evolution of Baby Boomers."

In 2011 Renee Chase wrote in her blog, Living Life My Way: "There was a time when I thought 50 was old but I was young and stupid back then and obviously my thoughts and opinions were stupid too. LOL!. I'm still the fun and silly kid I've always been, I'm just in an AWESOME Baby Boomer stage and I'm better than ever!"

Sometimes the appellation is tongue in cheek, especially when used by members of other generations. On the SurvivalistBoards website, "Aramchek" wrote in 2012: "I imagine only Boomer-age retirees will enjoy the fruits of SS, but they'll take it out of the hide of the young. They're already starting to do this, by raising the retirement age. What an 'awesome' generation the Boomers have been."

THE THIRTEENTH GENERATION, OR GENERATION X

(born 1961–1981)

To some generations much is given, as FDR said, and of others much is required. But there's a third possibility: a generation neither much-given-to nor much-required-of, but merely left to its own devices. Welcome to Generation X.

Strauss and Howe called it simply Generation 13, because it is the thirteenth by their count since what they called the Awakening Generation, born 1701–1723. They note that 13 has a certain aptness as being unlucky, and they argue that, in comparison with its Boomer predecessors, Generation 13 wasn't lucky in its nurturing. But the name that has come into widest use for this generation is similarly bleak: Generation X.

The term *Generation X* was originally generic, applicable to any generation. In that way it was much like *D-Day*, which until June 6, 1944, was known only as the designation for the first day of any military operation. By using *D-Day* instead of an actual date, schedulers could plan an operation without revealing when it would happen and without changing the designation if the event was postponed. D-Day for the Allied invasion of Normandy is an example. Bad weather postponed the invasion by a day, but there was no need to change the designation. The invasion of Normandy was such a major event that it has been known as D-Day ever since. It is the D-Day of D-days.

Likewise, Generation X is the Generation X of generations. It was originally the designation for any emerging generation. When a generation is starting out, like the current Homeland generation, born in 2005 and after, there's no way of telling exactly how it will develop. Hence *Generation X*, the X standing for the unknown.

That name was originally applied to several different generations coming into their own after World War II. Apparently the first to use *Generation X* for a new generation of unknown qualities was photographer Robert Capa. He applied it to the generation growing up after World War II, later to be known in the United States as Boomers. Then in the 1960s Generation X became the term for disaffected British youth, expressed in the title of a sociology book in 1965 and the name of a punk band in the 1970s.

But it was Douglas Coupland, a Canadian, who first applied the name to the American (and Canadian) generation that came in the wake of the Boomers. It was a generation so adrift that the Generation X label stayed with it.

In 1991, when the oldest of this new generation were beginning to reach their 30s, Coupland characterized them for all time in his novel *Generation X: Tales for an Accelerated Culture*.

(To be sure, Coupland's Generation X begins and ends earlier than Strauss and Howe's. He starts Generation X around 1957 and ends it a decade later. In his view it's followed by a "Global Teen" cohort, also lasting about a decade. His Generation X is approximately 1957–1967 and Global Teen 1966–1982, the two together approximately spanning Strauss and Howe's Generation 13.)

MCJOB AND LESSNESS

The Generation Xers of Coupland's novel were born around 1960, the first of the post-Boom generation. Three of his characters, in their early thirties, from Toronto, Los Angeles, and Portland, live in a rented bungalow in Palm Springs, California. They are the anti-Boomers, working at *McJobs* and escaping mainstream culture as best they can.

An acquaintance their age comes to visit, and the narrator says, "I realize that Tobias, in spite of his mask, is *shin jin rui*—X generation—just like us." And Tobias says: "To be honest, trying to look like a yuppie is pretty exhausting. I think I might even give up the whole ruse—there's no payoff. I might *even* become a bohemian like *these three*. Maybe move into a cardboard box on top of the RCA building; stop eating protein; work as live bait at Gator World. Why, I might *even move out here to the desert*."

Not only did Coupland affix a permanent label to this generation, he also supplied it with vocabulary. The margins of his illustrated book include close to a hundred definitions of words and phrases pertaining to Generation X, including many evidently of his own devising. Most were too odd or clever to enter the general vocabulary, but they set the tone. A picture of this generation emerges in his definitions:

Successophobia: The fear that if one is successful, then one's personal needs will be forgotten and one will no longer have one's childish needs catered to.

Emallgration: Migration toward lower-tech, lower-information environments containing a lessened emphasis on consumerism.

Lessness: A philosophy whereby one reconciles oneself with diminishing expectations of material wealth.

Decade blending: In clothing: the indiscriminate combination of two or more items from various decades to create a personal mood: *Sheila = Mary Quant earrings (1960s) + cork wedgie platform shoes (1970s) + black leather jacket (1950s and 1980s).*

Strauss and Howe make similar judgments about this new generation: "Like the music many of them listen to, 13ers can appear shocking on the outside, unknowable on the inside. Elders find it hard to suppress feelings of disappointment over how they are turning out—dismissing them as a 'lost,' 'ruined,' even 'wasted' generation in an unrelenting (and mostly unanswered) flurry of what Ellen Goodman has termed 'youth-bashing.'"

Coupland provides Generation X definitions in response to such criticisms.

Boomer envy: Envy of material wealth and long-range material security accrued by older members of the baby boom generation by virtue of fortunate births.

Clique maintenance: The need of one generation to see the generation following it as deficient so as to bolster its own collective ego: "Kids today do nothing. They're so apathetic. We used to go out and protest. All they do is shop and complain."

MTV GENERATION AND NINTENDO GENERATION

Technology touched the lives of Generation X, though not nearly as radically as it would for the Millennials who were to follow. Perhaps the most significant technological influence on Generation X was the cable channel MTV, Music Television, which began broadcasting on August 1, 1981, when many 13ers were in their teens. Because of MTV, pictures became almost as important as sounds for popular music, as they did for messaging in the next century. Videogames also first made their appearance when Generation Xers were young. Columnist Clarence Page suggested calling them the Nintendo Generation.

GENERATION A

Novelist Kurt Vonnegut proposed moving Generation X to the top of the alphabet in a 1994 commencement address at Syracuse University:

> *Now you young twerps want a new name for your generation? Probably not, you just want jobs, right? Well, the media do us all such tremendous favors when they call you Generation X, right? Two clicks from the very end of the alphabet. I hereby declare you Generation A, as much at the beginning of a series of astonishing triumphs and failures as Adam and Eve were so long ago.*
>
> *I apologize. I said I would apologize; I apologize now. I apologize because of the terrible mess the planet is in. But it has always been a mess. There have never been any "Good Old Days," there have just been days. And as I say to my grandchildren, "Don't look at me. I just got here myself."*
>
> *So you know what I'm going to do? I declare everybody here a member of Generation A. Tomorrow is another day for all of us.*

Predictably, nobody took Vonnegut's suggestion. In 2009, though, Coupland used it for the generation after Generation X, in a novel titled *Generation A*. But that's another story. To this day, Generation X remains two clicks from the end of the alphabet.

GENERATION LATCHKEY

Boomers more often than not had mothers at home when they returned from their day at school. Generation X wasn't always so supervised. Theirs was the first "divorce generation," where parents divorced at an unprecedented rate, leaving many of the new generation unsupervised in single-parent homes. As a result, some estimate that about 40 percent of Generation X at one time or another were *latchkey kids*.

True, Generation X was not the first to grow up in substantial numbers as latchkey kids. During World War II, especially, there were many households with absent fathers and working mothers where children carried house keys to let themselves in while adults were gone. And *latchkey* itself is an old-fashioned term, going back at least to the early 19th century when doors had latches instead of modern locks.

SLACKER

Generation X had its own version of the rebel. Where Boomers had their *hippies*, the counter-culture role in Generation X was the *slacker*, exemplified by Coupland's dropouts, and portrayed in Richard Linklater's 1991 movie *Slackers*. In that movie there are no stars, not even names for the characters. It's just a day in the life of slackers in Austin, Texas. The camera wanders from one scene to the next, following a different character each time. And the characters aren't identified by name, just by their attributes. To illustrate the slacker attitude, here is some of their dialogue:

WORKING ON SAME PAINTING: Sorry, I'm late.

HAVING A BREAKTHROUGH DAY: That's okay, time doesn't exist.

VIDEO INTERVIEWER: So, did you vote in the most recent election?

HITCHHIKER: Hell, no. I've got less important things to do.

DOSTOYEVSKY WANNABE: Who's ever written a great work about the immense effort required in order not to create?

DAIRY QUEEN PHOTOGRAPHER: So, what? Do you fancy yourself as some sort of artist or what?

ANTI-ARTIST: No, I'm an anti-artist.

DAIRY QUEEN PHOTOGRAPHER: Oooooh, one of those neo-poseur types that hangs out in coffee shops, and—doesn't do much of anything. Yeah.

T-SHIRT TERRORIST: Remember, terrorism is the surgical strike capability of the oppressed. Keep on keepin' on!

Slacker wasn't a brand-new designation. Back as far as World War I there had been *slackers*, men who preferred not to fight. But Generation X infused the word with a whole outlook on life.

GRUNGE

Grunge was an attitude before it was music, and the attitude was that of a slacker. As "krtdive" explains it in Urbandictionary:

- *Strive for apathy and underachiement*
- *Act like you dont care, even if you do*
- *Usually have cynnical and negative outlooks upon life*
- *Respect women and reject jocks*

Grunge was already in use in the 1960s to mean either "a slovenly or offensive person" or "grease, grime, or filth; anything nasty or inferior," as the *Historical Dictionary of American Slang* has it. But it was Generation X that brought it to prominence, setting it to music in the 1990s with "grunge bands" like Nirvana and Soundgarden. The music was "characterized by a sludgy guitar sound that uses a high level of distortion," says Wikipedia. Nirvana, in particular, led by Kurt Cobain, produced notable and provocative songs like "Smells Like Teen Spirit," "Aneurism," "Rape Me," and "Lithium."

"Lithium" begins like this:

I'm so happy cause today
I found my friends they're in my head
I'm so ugly, that's OK, cause so are you
We broke our mirrors

"Kurt Cobain's 1994 suicide was the JFK moment of my generation," recalls a Generation Xer who was twenty years old at the time of Cobain's death; "that and Rodney King, of course." When Cobain died at age twenty-seven, the short-lived dominance of grunge music soon came to an end.

HACKER

Generation X didn't grow up with email, texting, and the Internet. But in the 1990s while this generation still was young, some just in their teens, they eagerly embraced computer connections as they were being developed. The term *hacker* apparently had its origin in the 1950s at M.I.T. to designate people obsessed with machinery and then particularly computers. But it remained a local term until computer networks proliferated.

As long ago as 1972, when the oldest of Generation X were not yet teens, Stewart Brand, a member of the Silent Generation, offered this explanation in *Rolling Stone*: "A true hacker is not a group person. He's a person who loves to stay up all night, he and the machine in a love-hate relationship." By the 1990s, no explanation of *hacker* was needed.

As the term spread among Generation X, *hacker* acquired connotations of outlawry. The hacker's irreverent attitude toward the Internet and World Wide Web led some to be invaders of computer networks. The first two citations for *hacker* in the *Oxford English Dictionary* illustrate their mischievousness, or worse:

> *A gang of 23 teen-age computer hackers has done "sig-nificant damage" to Chase Manhattan Bank's records.*—
> USA Today, *October 18, 1985.*
>
> *Just for fun, the hackers decided to drop a few APBs (All Points Bulletins) into the local police computer, with the result that, when out driving in his car, he was repeat-edly stopped.*—TeleLink, *September–October 1986.*

Also in the 1990s, malicious hackers invented *phishing*, dan-gling bait in the form of email messages aimed at getting naïve users to reveal personal information, including bank account and credit card numbers.

GEEK

Nor did Generation X invent the *geek*. They just perfected him (or her).

As a slang term for a guy who isn't very impressive, *geek* has been around since the 19th century. A word-list compiled in 1911 by students at the University of Nebraska defined *geke* as "Awkward fellow, guy," with the example, "Isn't that fellow a queer, crazy geke?" Forty years later Nelson Algren wrote of a locale in Chicago, "The jungle hiders come softly forth: geeks and gargoyles, old blown winos, sour stewbums and grinning gin-soaks." The *Surfing Almanac* of 1977 defined *geek* as "A beginner who is always in the way of experienced surfers."

At colleges, *geek* easily extended its meaning to "an unsociable or overdiligent student," or just "a studious classmate," to quote some lexicons of the later 20th century. The *Historical Dictionary of American Slang* has an example from 1987: "Once a math-team geek at the University of Washington, Seal is postponing his schooling to become an MTV veejay."

And then came the computer revolution, when geeks became the ones with the esoteric knowledge, power, and wealth. It paid in more than one way to be a geek.

Douglas Coupland was again in the midst of Generation X action with his 1995 novel *Microserfs*, about computer programmers at Microsoft, back in the day when Microsoft was the unquestioned apex of the computer revolution. The programmers are, of course, geeks, and they live in a geek house:

> *Yes, Karla moved in a month ago. We're an item.*
>
> *Todd, Abe, and I lugged her "ownables" from her geek house down the street up to our own geek house at the top of the cul-de-sac: futon and frame . . . cluster o' computers . . . U-Frame-It Ansel Adams print. . . . And then, once she installed herself in our home (*"Think of me as a software application"*) she announced that she was an expert in (*thank you, Lord . . .)* shiatsu massage!*

Being a geek could help in elementary school too, as shown by the title of Barbara Park's 1992 children' book, *Fourth-grade Geek for President*.

And humorist Dave Berry called himself "a self-professed computer geek who actually does Windows 95" in 1996 when he published his book, *Dave Barry in Cyberspace*.

NERD

That brings us to *nerd*. It's essentially the same thing as *geek*, at least to Generation X and the Millennials. Not with so long a history, though. Evidence for its origin points to Dr. Seuss's 1950 children's story *If I Ran the* Zoo: "And then, just to show them, I'll sail to Ka-Troo. And Bring Back an IT-KUTCH, a PREEP and a PROO, a NERKLE, a NERD, and a SEERSUCKER, too!" His illustration of the nerd shows a shaggy-haired upright creature wearing a black T shirt.

There are other theories too. Just a year after Dr. Seuss's book was published, *Newsweek* in 1951 reported that "In Detroit, someone who once would be called a drip or a square is now, regrettably, a nerd."

Like *geek, nerd* was not at first a term of endearment, but the digital revolution ascribed new power and prestige to the fanatically studious who had no time to waste on social niceties. The *Oxford English Dictionary* captured one 1993 effort at distinguishing between the two words: "Geek is the proud, insider term for nerd. If you are not a dedicated techie, don't use this word."

DORK

You can add *dork* to the mix too, except that unlike *geek* and *nerd*, it doesn't have a redeeming connotation of computer expertise. John Sandford used it in his 1993 novel *Silent Prey*:

> *No sex, just sleeping together. Kennett laughing about it, but unhappy, too. His heart attack not that far past . . .*
>
> *"Hanging out with a geek," he said. "I can't believe it. I'm not enough, she's got a geek on the side."*
>
> *"Not a geek," she said.*
>
> *"All right. A dork. A nerd. Revenge of the Nerds, visited on Richard X. Kennett personally. A nerd may be dorking my woman. Or wait, maybe it's a dork is nerding my woman. . . ."*
>
> *"He's not a dork. He's really a nice guy."*

YOU GUYS

You guys is now the standard American plural of *you*. Well, the informal standard, at least. You won't find *you guys* in a presidential inaugural address, in a textbook (unless it quotes dialogue), or in solemn and serious prose. And in the South the alternative *y'all* is alive and well. But most of us nowadays address groups of people, especially people we know, as *you guys.* Not just men, but women too, and all ages.

We can thank lots of generations for this development—the Missionary Generation, who first put *you* and *guys* together in reference to men and boys; the Lost, who first occasionally applied it to women; the G.I.s, who spread it in World War II; Boomers, who took it up; Generation X, who distributed it widely; and Millennials, who unselfconsciously employed it for everyone. But perhaps we can thank Generation X for doing the most to let *you guys* hang out everywhere.

This most American of pronouns had an odd beginning, to say the least. It goes back to the name of a Frenchman, Guy Fawkes, notorious for having plotted to blow up the British houses of Parliament in 1605. The plot was foiled, and the anniversary of the day he was arrested, November 5, became a holiday in England and its colonies, where an effigy of Guy Fawkes would be burned in a bonfire.

By the mid-19th century, in American English, *guy* came to have a more neutral meaning, first a strange-looking straw effigy, then a strange-looking man, then just any man, a regular *guy.* By the mid-20th century, it was possible to refer to a woman as a "regular guy." Jonathan Lighter's *Historical Dictionary of American Slang* has this 1927 quote from a letter by Eugene O'Neil: "She is a 'real guy.' You'll like her immensely."

So from the late 19th century onward we have the plural pronoun *you guys*. But at that time it was mostly in a slangy context. A 1929 story in *Boys' Life*, "Hunters Two," begins, "What? Hunter's stew? No, no, you guys have got me all wrong. That ain't what I'm goin' to tell you about." Or take Damon Runyon, whose stories in slang inspired the musical *Guys and Dolls*. In a 1935 collection of his stories, one character says, "I suppose I owe you guys an apology for busting up your quartet when I toss those slugs at Louie the Lug?"

But it's different nowadays. *You guys* has become gender-blind. Admittedly, that doesn't sit too well with some members of older generations. Boomer Lori Borgman (born 1954), for example, writes in a 2005 collection of her newspaper columns:

> *A second, yet equally disturbing, trend in dining is the use of that ever popular phrase "you guys." I walk into a restaurant with female friends and the host or hostess says, "How are you guys today? Would you guys like a table or a booth? Can I get you guys something to drink?" The* you guys *phenomenon is even more puzzling than the announcement that a total stranger is going to be taking care of me today.*

Feminist writers of the Boomer generation, such as Alice Walker (born 1944) and Audrey Bolger (born 1960), object to *you guys* on the more serious grounds that it's sexist, but succeeding generations seem to pay that no mind.

A typical present-day instance is from the afterword of a nonfiction book, *A Mother's Love: One Families Experience with Leukemia and Their Son* (2008) by Rosalie Klein, a Generation Xer, where she writes with seven exclamation points, "I love you guys!!!!!!!"

LIKE

No, Generation X can't be credited with introducing *like* into the English language. It's been around, like, for centuries, as a verb (I *like* you guys) and a preposition (Just *like* that), among many other uses, and more recently in the language of jazz musicians and hipsters in the latter half of the 20th century as an interjection—"*Like*, that was so cool!" or "It was, *like*, all we could handle"—added to a sentence wherever you could insert a pause. From the *Valley Girls' Guide* of 1982, we get the definition: "*Like*—What you say when you're like, um, attaching one word to another, in a, like, sentence." At the University of Tennessee in 1987 a student wrote in a theme, "I was sitting down and like this nerd he like sits next to me and like I thought I was going to die!"

But it was Generation X who added the twist of using "like" to mean "say" or "think." For example:

"I was like, Mom?" "She was like, What!"

A man came up to me and said, "You really look like Princess Di."

And he looked at me and he's like, "Are you?"

It appears to have emerged from the "like"-saturated language affected by Generation X teenage girls of the San Fernando Valley in southern California. If anybody ever liked "like," it was the cool yet adorably clueless Valley Girls.

The Valley Girl language was satirized, and publicized, by Moon Unit Zappa and her father Frank Zappa in a 1982 song with the eponymous title "Valley Girl." In that song "like" butts in about thirty times, most often with no role except to mark the speaker as cool. But in one of the stanzas the Valley Girl declares:

So like I go into this like salon place, yknow
And I wanted like to get my toenails done
And the lady like goes, oh my god, your toenails
Are like so grody
It was like really embarrassing
She's like oh my god, like bag those toenails
I'm like sure
She goes, I don't know if I can handle this, y'know.
I was like really embarrassed.

Amid this thicket of "like"s we can detect two that show this new use, the "like" with a form of "be" taking the place of "say" or "think": "She's *like* oh my god, like bag those toenails" and the reply "I'm *like* sure." These are two of the earliest mutations of "like" to this new use.

Generation X bequeathed this "like" to the Millennials, who keep on liking like the rest of us. What began as a Valley Girl affectation has nowadays become a routine way of indicating thought or speech. An Internet example from 2012: "She was like, I can't confirm nor deny any clients that stay here. So we were like, we saw them so we can confirm it lol."

And here's actor Josh Hutcherson, talking in 2012 about an incident during the filming of *The Hunger Games*: "She [Jennifer Lawrence] was like, 'I can kick over your head,' and I was like, 'No you can't' and she went to kick over my head and ended up kicking me on the side of the head. She was crying and felt so bad, it was funny actually."

Here's a recent sample from Facebook:

> *So I was talking to my friend the other day and I was like, "So, like, what did you do on Saturday?" and she's like, "Not much. You?" And I'm like, "Yeah. Same thing." And she's like, "Fun." And then we were both like, "Wow."*

An Associated Press story in 2013 about the death of seventy-seven-year-old Robert Taylor, inventor of SoftSoap, included this reflection from his Generation X daughter: "He was just driving to work one day and he had been looking at the soap in the sink and seeing how messy it was and he was like, 'There's got to be a way to not have to deal with that.'"

But why has this "like" spread so widely among people who don't have the least trace of Valley in their speech? Why do so many of us make routine use of it now?

The answer could be that this use of "like" allows us to introduce not just *what* we said or thought, but *how*. Instead of merely saying the words, "like" with "be" allows us to enact the scene. It's an extension of a long-standing use of "like" to indicate manner: March came in *like a lion*, he raged *like a madman*. So "I was . . . like this" became "I was like . . . this," where "this" was a gesture or exclamation or both.

That's the difference between plain "I said I would" and "I was like, I would!" We need the latter for the moments when we want to show as well as tell.

Yes, the Valley Girls in Generation X did a really useful thing for the English language. They gave us a new function for an old word, a function so useful it has spread to all ages and around the world. Thanks, girls!

HEY

In the days before Generation X, most Americans outside the South greeted each other with *hi* if they didn't use the more formal *hello*. That was the situation in the late 1960s when the *Dictionary of American Regional English* sent interviewers to a thousand communities around the nation, asking (among 1,846 other things) how locals would greet somebody they knew well. The dictionary fieldworkers found sixty people who would say *hey*, mostly in the South and Lower Mississippi Valley. To illustrate the usage, that dictionary quotes Harper Lee's *To Kill a Mockingbird*, set in Alabama: "Tell him hey for me, won't you?" and the reply, "I'll tell him you said hey."

The *Dictionary of American Regional English* doesn't even have an entry for "hi," which evidently was too universal then to be a regional expression.

In those days, *hey* was so unusual outside the South that Willie Mays, a native of Alabama, was called the "Say Hey Kid" because he would say, "Hey, man. Say hey, man" to fellow ballplayers. In 1954 the saying even became a song, by the Treniers, with this refrain:

> *Say hey, say who?*
> *Say Willie*
> *Say hey, say who?*
> *Swinging at the plate*
> *Say hey, say who?*
> *Say Willie*
> *That Giants kid is great.*

Perhaps Mays was the one to raise awareness of *hey* as an alternative to *hi*. In any case, as Generation X grew up, *hey* began to expand beyond its former boundaries, emerging from the Old South to be a common expression for greeting friends and relatives. Google Ngrams shows *hi* dropping in frequency until about 1985, with *hey* slowly increasing after that, though to this day *hi* remains more frequent.

And Millennials have carried it even further. Cat Flynn, a Millennial, explains her usage: "With regards to *hi* versus *hey*, I almost always say *hey* in speech but I have free variation between *hi* and *hey* in writing. Actually it's a little more complicated than that since I have a sort of three-way formality distinction for greetings—*hey* for friends my own age or younger, *hi* for adults I know well or people my own age I'm just meeting, and *hello* for adult strangers."

ROAD TRIP

Generation X was restless. Their predecessors the Boomers tended to bloom where they were planted, but Generation X was less happy. When things were less than ideal at home, as they often were, they took off. To get away, and for adventure, they drove away on *road trips*.

Sometimes they would pick an arbitrary destination on a map and drive there in search of a soft drink, or maybe a hard one. Sometimes they wouldn't choose a destination at all but just go.

A road trip generally isn't a trip to get to a specific place. It's a drive for the sake of driving, with or without a specific destination. "Road tripping is much more than a way of travel—it's a way of life. It's all the unique, peak, and freak experiences you have along the way," says Cameron Tuttle in her 1999 book, *The Bad Girl's Guide to the Open Road*. "Road tripping is exploring back roads, cruising through the cracks and crevices of an America you can't read about in any book."

A member of Generation X in good standing, Gretchen Stauder, recently made a 200-mile road trip to visit a friend.

When the friend's nephew offered her a free kitten, she took it and named it Road Trip, Roady for short. That's the kind of impression the road trip made on her generation.

Of course, they weren't the first to take a drive just for the sake of driving. Jack Kerouac's *On the Road*, published in 1957 before any members of Generation X were born, was an inspiration and instigation for Boomer road tripping, but it was the members of X who were influenced most by his travels. Another inspiration was the 1969 biker movie *Easy Rider*.

HOOK UP

By far the most common uses of *hook up*, even today, are innocuous. A 1977 book called *Hook Up,* for example, has the subtitle *A Complete Guide to Southern California Ocean Sportfishing*. A 1984 book titles itself *Telemarketing: Hook-up to Higher Profits*. Another book with the title *Hook Up*, published in 1995, has the subtitle *Get Hired! The Internet Job Search Revolution*. You can "hook up" sections of track for a model railroad. But you can also use *hook up* for any kind of intimate interaction.

It was Generation X that increasingly gave *hook up* this more intimate meaning. Tom Wolfe took it to the extreme in his 2001 essay "Hooking Up":

> *"Hooking up" was a term known in the year 2000 to almost every American child over the age of nine*

[Generation X then ranged from 39 to 19, Millennials 18 to just born], but to only a relatively small percentage of their parents, who, even if they heard it, thought it was being used in the old sense of 'meeting' someone. Among the children, hooking up was always a sexual experience, but the nature and extent of what they did could vary widely.

Hooking up evidently flourishes today. So a story on alcohol and sexual assault in the *Chronicle of Higher Education's* daily blog for September 4, 2014, could begin with this matter-of-fact assertion: "At the beginning of every academic year, college freshmen are quickly introduced to two hallmarks of campus social life, drinking and hooking up."

Kathleen A. Bogle made a more moderate appraisal in her 2008 book *Hooking Up: Sex, Dating, and Relationships on Campus.* She says the term, whatever its implications, has been popular on college campuses ever since Generation X went to college. And it can mean something as innocuous as kissing, as well as much more. Perhaps *hooking up* has attained popularity exactly because it's ambiguous, just as relationships often are.

NO WAY – WAY

There's no way the language of a whole generation could be influenced by a clueless character on *Saturday Night Live*, right? Way!

Yes, the character was Wayne of SNL (and the movie *Wayne's World*), portrayed by Mike Myers, in the early 1990s. *No way* and *Way* always came out with great enthusiasm. One famous *Saturday Night Live* sketch in 1991 has Wayne making out with Madonna after this conversation:

MADONNA: Wayne, do you want to play Truth or Dare?
WAYNE: Truth or Dare? With me? No way.
MADONNA: Way.
WAYNE: No Way.
MADONNA: Way.
WAYNE: Excellent.

Way indeed became the way often enough in the '90s. Here's Douglas Coupland again, the chronicler of Generation X, in his 1993 novel *Shampoo Planet*: "By the way, Jasmine. Guess what? You've become the cult Halloween costume for this year." "No way." "Way. Everyone at school is planning to go dressed as Jasmine Johnson and write stuff on their foreheads." "Out!"

And here's a bit of dialogue from *The Lemon Chicken Jones: A Saxon Mystery* by Les Roberts (1994): " 'So let me come along.' 'No way.' 'Way!' he said. He'd been watching too much *Saturday Night Live*."

WHATEVER

But the signature expression of Generation X is *Whatever!* Not the routine pronoun that has been in the English language for a good seven centuries, but the interjection that is a complete declaration in itself. Sometimes, as in the 1995 movie *Clueless*, made when the last of Generation X were in high school, it was accompanied by a W gesture, thumbs together, forefingers forming a V on each hand.

And it lives on. "*Whatever* is the catchphrase of Gen X," said a member of that generation on Yahoo Answers in 2012. "Gen Y can't steal that from us."

Speaking for Generation X, Mat Honan declared on his blog in 2011: "Generation X is used to being ignored, stuffed between two much larger, much more vocal, demographics. But whatever! Generation X is self-sufficient."

FUN

Still, all was not gloom for Generation X. They had fun too—so much fun that they were the first to embrace *fun* as an adjective, as in "We had a fun time." Until Generation X came along, *fun* was perfectly well known but just as a noun, as in "We had fun."

And it has crept into general acceptance, at least among the young. On Twitter nowadays you can find, "making a very fun purchase today," "that was a very fun 1 minute skype call," "I don't talk a lot and I'm not the very fun type either," "Utsugi Sensei gave a very fun and educational workshop on the art of Kabuki this morning in year 9."

THE MILLENNIAL GENERATION, OR GENERATION Y

(born 1982–2004)

As the 20th century drew to an end, the naming and characterizing of generations had become a significant enterprise. No longer was it merely a matter of looking back on generations come and gone. This time numerous self-appointed experts vied to be first to give a name to the generation that began to be born in 1982.

In 1990, when the oldest members of the new generation were barely eight, it would seem too early to predict their characteristics ten or twenty years hence. No matter; Strauss and Howe played it safe by calling them the Millennial Generation. That was a sure bet. Whatever else, those born 1982 and after would be the first to reach adulthood in the 21st century and first to have a few members born in the new millennium as well.

But as Strauss and Howe surely intended, "Millennial" has connotations beyond chronological. The millennium, in another sense, is a grand climax, a time of great events, and they foresaw that their Millennial Generation would be up to the challenge and the opportunity. In their 1997 book *The Fourth Turning*, Strauss and Howe predicted a "Crisis . . . around the year 2005, then the climax . . . around 2020, the resolution around 2026." And who will get us through this crisis to the happy millennium? None other than "the young-adult Heroes," members of the generation they called Millennial.

As early as 1990, with more than half of the Millennials yet unborn, the authors of *Generations* ventured to characterize them in ten detailed pages, summarized as: "Cute. Cheerful. Scoutlike. Wanted." This Millennial generation, they said, "is being treated as precious." Indeed, their Boomer parents soon acquired the reputation of "helicopter parents."

More recently, Howe has characterized the Millennials as "special, sheltered, confident, team oriented, conventional, pressured, and achieving." And thus, he says, they feel entitled.

Looking at the Millennials now, a quarter of a century later, we can indeed say they feel entitled. They have been gifted with unprecedented technological innovations to help them make their mark on each other and the world. And they are happy to present themselves to the world, online and in selfies, as the next best thing.

GENERATION Y

As successors to Generation X, they have often been labeled *Generation Y*. But that designation has little suggestive power. When the new generation began to come under discussion, both *Generation Y* and *Millennials* were widely used, but perhaps because of the suggestiveness of Strauss and Howe's term, since the mid-'90s *Millennials* has become the usual designation.

ECHO BOOMERS

They have also been called Echo Boomers because of a boom of births that began in the 1980s, a smaller echo of the postwar baby boom. Echo Boomers characterizes their numbers, but not their attitudes. Strauss and Howe argue that the Millennials will be less like their Boomer parents and more like the heroic G.I. Generation.

In 1998 *USA Today* proclaimed: "Call them Generation Y, Millennials, Echo Boomers or Generation 2000. By any name, they are the coddled, confident offspring of post-World War II baby boomers."

GENERATION I, GENERATION N, GENERATION WWW, GENERATION FACEBOOK

Still other names have been proposed. It should be Generation I, Bill Gates said in 1999, since it was the first generation to grow up with the Internet. Others called it Generation Net or Gen N for the same reason. In 1997, *Time* nicknamed it Generation WWW. More recently, with some justification, it has been called Generation Facebook, the first to encounter and embrace social media. They were the first to *friend* and *unfriend* over the Internet, thanks to the invention of Facebook by Mark Zuckerberg (born 1984), one of their own.

In a word (or prefix), Millennials can indeed be called the first fully *i* generation. Introducing the iMac computer in 1998, when the first of the Millennials were entering college, Boomer Steve Jobs associated *i* with the words *Internet, individual, instruct, inform,* and *inspire.* In the following decade Jobs inspired the Millennials with his iPod, iPhone, and iPad.

And the Internet is where the language of the Millennials can be found. Previous generations spent their youth communicating the old-fashioned way, on paper, by phone, and even face to face, but the natural medium for Millennials is texts and tweets and selfies. More than any previous generation, they write instead of talking. Even phone calls are so 20th century.

They have their own dictionary, too. Millennials don't bother to check what *Merriam-Webster* says; they write their own definitions at Urbandictionary.com, where they are posted for all to see and then vote on. On that website most words have at least several competing definitions, if not dozens, and Urbandictionary.com ranks them by vote, the most preferred first.

Because their communication depends so much on technology, many words in the Millennial vocabulary could not be invented until the technology was invented that made them possible. Millennials had to wait for the invention of Facebook (2004) and Twitter (2006) before they could *friend* or *unfriend* or end a message with a *hashtag*. And it took the invention of the iPhone 4 (2010) with its front-facing camera to make *selfies* possible.

FOMO

With all the virtual worlds at their fingertips, Millennials have come up with a new ailment that now is afflicting other generations too: FOMO, or fear of missing out. Social media now make it possible for our friends and acquaintances to tell us instantly and 24/7 the exciting things they're doing. So Millennials are constantly aware of the good times others are having while they, for example, might just be home alone on a Saturday night. That's FOMO.

In days gone by, phone calls and snail mail were the principal alternatives to face-to-face communication. Nowadays there are also IM, Facebook, Twitter, Instagram, Snapchat and the like for personal messages, and endless blogs and websites to watch on the Internet. Instant communication is so important that often, at a happening event, Millennials will be busy texting others who aren't there rather than interacting with those who are. And everyone is less happy.

So of course the Internet offers advice on how to combat FOMO. The "Art of Manliness" website tells FOMO sufferers to ask themselves: "Is this something I really wished I was doing?" "Is this feeling telling me something I need to change?" "Is this something that is viable for me right now?" and perhaps most important, "Is this an accurate representation of reality?" Maybe other lives are not as rosy as they are portrayed.

SELFIE

In 2013 there emerged a word that managed to portray the essence of Millennials, evoking their world and their world view in just two syllables: *selfie*. Along with its lesser known antithesis, the *unselfie*, and other derivatives like *shelfie* (a picture of one's books) and *theftie* (a picture of the thief of one's cellphone, taken automatically when the thief first tries to use it), *selfie* reflects the Millennials' immersion in technology and social media; lives sometimes lived more comfortably online than in person; concern for their image; and generosity in offering their best selves to friends and the world. For

Millennials, the selfie is the conjunction of technology with desire.

Self-portraits have existed forever, of course, but selfies are relatively new. The word itself is barely a decade old. And for it to become a fave of the Millennials happened later than that, because it required technology that wasn't available until Steve Jobs introduced the iPhone 4 in 2010. To the camera on the back of earlier iPhones, the 4 added a camera in front, allowing users to hold their phones at arm's length and check their poses onscreen before taking a picture. Other smartphones followed that lead, of course, and now it's a standard feature of any decent 21st-century phone.

Just taking a picture isn't enough to make it a true selfie. You have to send it. So the technology of social media also was needed, making it easy not only to take pictures of the self but also to send them. Facebook has been the dominant medium for selfies, but now there's Twitter and Instragram and Snapchat too, among others.

You can pose yourself in different ways for different effects. Your selfie can be a closeup of your face or a not-so-closeup of your body. You can pose yourself good-looking, well dressed, or not much dressed at all. You can also make a face—a kissy face or a duck face, as well as a smile or a frown. You can take a selfie of yourself with someone else, a friend or a celebrity or a friend who is a celebrity. You can use a *selfie stick* to hold your camera further away, to get a more panoramic picture. And you can have someone else take a selfie of yourself holding your camera and making a selfie of yourself.

Yes, and celebrities take selfies too, and not just Millennial celebrities either; the president of the United States has been known to indulge. It's celebrated also by the doting daughter of a non-celebrity who tweeted, "My daddy takes selfies bc he's awesome like that #daddysgirl #selfie#mountains #parentstext #cabinpic."

Selfie itself is an almost perfect word. It's transparently about the self. It's selfish, but the diminutive suffix -*ie* makes it cute selfish instead of mean selfish. And it is quite literally a self expression, in both senses of that term. For the Millennials, it's a gift of their self to the watching world.

Despite its indulgent narcissism, the selfie can easily take a turn for the good. This happened, for example, in the aftermath of a devastating typhoon that damaged the Philippines in 2013. Young people began posting *unselfies*, pictures of themselves holding signs with addresses of websites that accepted donations for relief.

Likewise, the #GivingTuesday movement, seeking charitable donations on the Tuesday after Thanksgiving and after the shopping days of Black Friday and Cyber Monday, encouraged the use of #unselfie for messages promoting its program.

In the *Huffington Post* for November 22, 2013, Jeffrey Walker wrote, "Let's turn that [selfie] trend, and everyone's cameras, around and start taking 'UNselfie' pictures. These 'UNselfie' pictures could be of people doing good things, of acts of kindness, of compassion in action! Being UNselfish!"

The Millennial version of Generation X's Valley Girls was both celebrated and satirized in 2014 in the wildly popular song "#Selfie" (using the hashtag, of course) by two guys known as the Chainsmokers. It's a monologue spoken (not sung) to girlfriends at a club, by a girl who is concerned about what a possible boyfriend is doing. She sends selfies to get his attention, meanwhile constantly seeking approval and validation from her friends. The full effect requires the YouTube video, but the attitudes are clearly expressed in the lyrics:

> *Let me take a selfie.... Can you guys help me pick a filter? . . . I wanna look tan.*
>
> *What should my caption be? I want it to be clever. How about "Livin' with my bitches, #Liv."*
>
> *I only got ten likes in the last five minutes. Do you think I should take it down? Let me take another selfie.*
>
> *Wait, pause, Jason just liked my selfie.... Is that guy sleeping over there? Yeah, the one next to the girl with no shoes on. That's so ratchet....*
>
> *Oh my god, Jason just texted me. Should I go home with him? I guess I took a good selfie. Let me take a selfie.*

"#Liv" refers to Club Liv, P. Diddy's club in Miami, where the Chainsmokers were performing when they first produced

"#Selfie." (And "ratchet" is a not so complimentary term for a young woman who is less attractive than she thinks.)

As if that hit video weren't enough, "Selfie" became a half-hour comedy series on ABC television in Fall 2014. "Can a self-absorbed social media diva learn how to live life offline?" asked ABC. "Follow Eliza Dooley on her quest to trade in digital relationships for real ones." Only a Millennial would have that problem. For some reason, however, the show didn't catch on: it was canceled in less than two months.

EDM

Who needs musicians to make a hit? Or musical instruments? Or singers? The video of "Selfie" is a prime example of the recent Millennial fad known as EDM, short for Electronic Dance Music. It's music meant for dancing (also a Millennial fad). But the distinctive thing about this generation's music is that it doesn't need musicians. EDM is produced not by live bands but by DJs like the Chainsmokers, who mix rhythmical sounds to make something insistent to dance to. Not everyone calls it music, but it does get Millennials dancing. The Chainsmokers draw large crowds when they tour. Their website explains: "With live sets and productions that their own mother describe as, 'sounds nice, but a little loud,' these two always put on a show that was not ever described as sexy and life-changing, but should be."

HIPSTER

Not every Millennial dances to EDM. At the opposite end of the Millennial spectrum, there are *hipsters.*

Boomers had hippies; the Echo Boomers have hipsters. What's the difference?

Hip, with the meaning "to be in the know," is common to all generations beginning with the Lost, born in the late 19th century. Even today we're all hip to that word, as in the headline of a recent post on the website of the *Chronicle of Higher Education*: "The Next 'Hip' Question in Admissions?"

But *hipster* is different. It was used by the Silent Generation, then retired as the *hippies* of the Boom Generation became young adults, and then revived in the language of the Millennials, different from before.

The present-day *hipster* isn't destroyed by drugs like the hipster of Allen Ginsberg's Silent Generation, but also isn't the Boomers' mellow hippie. Instead, the *hipster* is lean and ascetic, subversive and ironic, and wears tight pants.

According to the first definition in Urban Dictionary, "Hipsters are a subculture of men and women typically in their 20's and 30's that value independent thinking, counter-culture, progressive politics, an appreciation of art and indie-rock, creativity, intelligence, and witty banter . . . Hipsters reject the culturally-ignorant attitudes of mainstream consumers, and are often seen wearing vintage and thrift store inspired fashions, tight-fitting jeans, old-school sneakers, and sometimes thick rimmed glasses. Both hipster men and women sport similar androgynous hair styles that include combinations of messy shag cuts and asymmetric side-swept bangs."

The website LOL I'm a Hipster offers an eighteen-step program in "How to Be a Modern Hipster," including "Be thin and get rid of your acne," "Smoke weed" but "Don't be a pothead," "Be green and a vegetarian/vegan," and "Refuse to write in anything but Moleskines."

Wired magazine takes a different look at modern hipsters in a 2011 review:

> *With a starting list price at a little under $16,000, the iQ continues Scion's reputation for making inexpensive, funky-looking cars for young urbanites.*
>
> *Hipsters need music, so the iQ comes standard with a 160-watt, four-speaker Pioneer audio system with an AM/FM radio, CD player, a USB port, HD radio and a built-in hands-free phone connection with streaming audio capability.*

Not everyone is so impressed. Joe Queenan, for example, in a 2013 article in the *Wall Street Journal*, lamented "the official hipster uniform. Red sneakers. Natty fedoras. No socks. Statement scarves unfurled long after winter has passed. Orlon shirts. Watch caps worn by those who have never watched anything. The whole 'Revenge of the Nerds' package."

That look is old, as Queenan explains. "Cheap plastic shades as an ironic statement go back to John Belushi. Self-parodying Clark Kent glasses date back at least as far as Elvis Costello, circa 1976, already channeling Buddy Holly, circa 1956. Wearing a tuxedo with running shoes is a seditious look that Garrison Keillor introduced during the Reagan administration." And he mentions "skinny jeans with penny loafers, oversize aviator glasses and self-conscious preppy regalia."

Ted Benson, a graduate student at M.I.T., offered this description of the hipster in a *Chronicle of Higher Education* post in 2013:

> *Readers of a certain age may still associate hipsters with aficionados of 1940s bebop. But today's version is a different postmodern animal, demonstrating coolness by cultivating tastes and habits that run counter to prevailing consumer-culture norms.*
>
> *By those standards, an ugly Christmas sweater, a mustache, and $1.99 neon-plastic sunglasses aren't kitschy, they're cool, because they reject the mass-media notion that we should look like Calvin Klein models. Watery beer, white bread, and processed cheese singles make for a romantic first date. The more you show the world you don't care about its expectations, the higher you've climbed on the hipster ladder.*

So much for the hipster look. When the Homeland Generation generates its own version of counter-culture rebels, will they be a new incarnation of hippies?

AWKWARD

Who would have thought it? Millennials are awkward.

Or so they say. Often.

Maybe it's because they spend so much time online that they haven't had enough practice in social skills to avoid awkwardness when they're face to face. Or maybe they make so much of awkwardness because they want to assure each other that social niceties don't matter to members of their generation. They are too busy multitasking via text, Facebook, Instagram, Snapchat, and email, as well as via voice and f2f, that they can't take the time to develop the skills that were expected when voice and f2f and letter were the only ways to interact.

Maria Yagoda, a recent college graduate, explained it this way in her father's blog post: "Youth culture needed a word to embody the discomfort that comes along with the extreme awareness of ourselves, and how others perceive us, that we experience in our day-to-day lives. My generation can't handle lulls; with all our various forms of communication, we're too quick and self-aware for social glitches to go unnoticed and unaddressed."

Whatever the reason, Millennials are the generation that actually says "awkward" when a situation is awkward. The word is so notable that it has evoked 67 different definitions on Urbandictionary.com, including this one:

> *A common word overused by kids in junior high, almost in the same group with "LOL" and "random!" Used to try*

> *and impress your preteen friends after or during a long*
> *pause between conversations. Also used by idiots when-*
> *ever there is a pause in speech. Sometimes accompanied*
> *by a hand motion resembling a turtle or a turkey.*

TEEN 1: . . . and that's what I did last Saturday!

TEENS 2, 3, AND 4: . . . okay. . .

silence

TEEN 5: . . . aaaaawkwardddd. . .

What's that hand motion resembling a turtle? Well, it adds to and proclaims awkwardness. You hold your hands in front of you, one on top of the other, palms down, and wiggle your thumbs to suggest a turtle crawling or swimming. Awkward indeed!

Jane Solomon, a Millennial no longer in her teens, explained: "Everyone in my generation feels awkward at parties. Even the people who look like they're having the most fun." And she noted a connection to the hipster: "There's a sort of hipness to being awkward. It's cool to have been an awkward kid, if that makes any sense. Hipster culture is very much about being dorky and awkward."

ABBREVS

As the Millennial Generation grew up, they indulged in new versions of telegraphese, inspired by the new technology of texting and tweeting. Abbreviations had been the rage before, whether encouraged by the cost of sending telegraph messages and telegrams, or just by foolishness, like the fad for abbreviations in Boston in the 1830s that led to the invention of O.K. In the computer age, new abbreviations were born.

But it's not just in texting or tweeting that abbrevs characterize the communications of the Millennials. They also carry over abbrev style in f2f conversations, perhaps reflecting the dominant reality of social media. Even when you're sitting next to a friend, why speak when you can text? It's especially teenage girls who say "legit," "jeal," and "quest" in conversation.

On Facebook, there's a group called "The Abbrevs," founded in 2009, that takes as its mission

> *To spread the art of abbrev-ing throughout society and to prom (abbrev: promote) peace and love, as well as remind people that abbrevs and acs (abbrev: acronyms) are TD . . . tot diff (TD = acronym for Totally Different; tot diff = abbrev for Totally Different).*

In September 2012, The Abbrevs page had more than 500 likes.

In January 2010, Colleen Bruce posted this appreciation on The Abbrevs:

> *You're my fave fan group ev. I always use abreevs. I use them evday. Pretty much in ev conv i have. Me and my fam use them all the time. It's prett unbeliev if you ask for my opin. Peop (people) are us (usually) prett jel of me and my lang.*

The late William Safire, pundit and language columnist, observed in 2009:

> *Today, the* fave *(for "favorite") abbreves are* obvi *(a shortening of 'Thank you, Captain Obvious') and* belig *(a clipping of "belligerent," retaining the soft* g*). Nobody in the young-barflies crowd orders "the usual"; it's the* yoozh. *My grandnephew Jesse concludes sentences with* whatev, *which is* probs *(for "probably") "whatever." In this cacophony of abbreves, word endings are scattered all over the floor. Go* fig.

LOL

Among the abbrevs, LOL stands out. Cat Flynn, a 2013 graduate of Cornell University, offers this personal history of a versatile and elusive word:

> *I remember stuff like LOL (which, by the way, I hear far more often pronounced as a single word rhyming with "crawl" rather than el-oh-el) as early as circa 1998 when I first started using AOL Instant Messenger with my friends from elementary school. In fact I remember the first time I ever saw someone use "lol" I was confused since I thought it was an abbreviation of "lollipop."*

"Lol" has also undergone semantic drift in that it almost never means "laughing out loud" unless it's used by someone of an older generation who didn't grow up with the Internet; people my age generally go "BAHAHAHAHAHAHA" to represent laughing (and sometimes even deliberately exaggerated phrases like "SCREAMING" or "THERE ARE TEARS IN MY EYES" to evoke extreme, convulsive laughter—also phrases in asterisks like *snorting* are a recent development) while "lol," sometimes spelled "lawl," generally means "Haha that's so funny. NOT." and is generally very sarcastic. So things have kind of come full circle since a lot of social media, Twitter aside, no longer have character limits so abbreviations, at least older ones, are often interpreted sarcastically due to being seen as passé.

YOLO

Among her "Seven Reasons Why Boomer Women Are Better," Stacy Doyle declared:

> *Did you ever hear a young woman says something like, "I got merked [put down, trashed] at the party last night, it was cray-cray. Oh well, YOLO." There's just too*

> *much interpretation involved in a regular conversation.*
> *Another bonus—boomer women talk rather than text.*
> *Most of us still can't make our fingers type on those tiny*
> *buttons on a cell phone.*
>
> > *Well, you only live once. YOLO!*

This not so original observation went viral in 2011, in the wake of a song "The Motto" by the rapper Drake that put a positive spin on clubs, sex, drugs, and money, in blunt terms like these:

> *You only live once—that's the motto nigga YOLO. And*
> *we 'bout it every day, every day, every day. Like we sit-*
> *ting on the bench, nigga we don't really play.*

Since then, #YOLO has become a comment on anything foolish. It's excoriated in Urbandictionary, where its most popular definition goes like this:

The dumbass's excuse for something stupid that they did. Also one of the most annoying abbreviations ever. . . .

GUY 1: "Hey i heard that you broke ur leg falling off the balcony at that party"

DUMBASS 1: "Ya but hey YOLO"

And the group Lonely Island takes the same attitude in its song YOLO, with verses like:

Ugh, you only live once, that's the motto. So take a chill
pill, ease off the throttle. Never go to loud clubs cause
it's bad for your ears. Your friends will all be sorry when
they can't hear.

HASHTAG

Hashtags seem so ordinary now, but within recent memory nobody even knew about them, let alone used them. True, for decades some computer programmers had used #, the hash (or pound, or number) sign, for designating topics and groups. But it was the advent of Twitter in 2006 that within a few years made the hashtag universal. The story goes that in 2007 open-source advocate Chris Messina was the first to attach to a tweet # followed by a topic. Within a few years, one or more hashtags became the familiar accompaniment of a tweet, designating both topics and comments. The hashtag was a revolutionary user-generated way of organizing the Internet, of providing a context, a classification, a comment for any statement. Or maybe all three, as in this tweet from May 14, 2014: This is too funny #Jayz #Solange #Beyonce #Fight #Elevator.

By 2012 *hashtag* was so pervasive and significant that the American Dialect Society chose it as word of the year.

Messina was born in 1981, the last birth year of Generation X, but it was the younger Millennials who most enthusiastically embraced tweets and hashtags, although older celebrities, politicians, and pundits also happily joined in.

WEIRD

It's weird, but "weird" is a word peculiarly favored by Millennials. Maybe because, in the words of a 2012 tweet by a "24-year-old blogger extraordinaire" named Rayanne Forbes, "Being called weird is like being called limited edition; meaning you're something people don't see that often. Remember that." She hashtagged her tweet #weird&proud.

Weird has plenty of synonyms: strange, odd, creepy, bizarre, and freaky, among others studied recently by Sali Tagliamonte and her students at the University of Toronto. They reported that "*strange, odd, unusual*, the older forms, are favoured by the elderly speakers while the rising form *weird*, which was not attested until 1817, is favoured by those under 40."

For Millennials, *weird* can have positive connotations. An entry posted on Urbandictionary in 2008 explains that weird can mean "out of the ordinary" and "unusual but in a good way," with this conversation:

PERSON 1: how are you?
PERSON 2: extrasuperfantastic
PERSON 3: you are so weird!

MEH

Millennials aren't interested in what they aren't interested in. And they have an expression for it: "meh."

There's no mystery where "meh" comes from. It was expressed, and even spelled out, in episodes of *The Simpsons,* which could be considered the ultimate Millennial TV show, having been with the Millennials since the oldest of them were barely eight. At first, when the Simpson daughter, Lisa, used it in 1992, it was hardly more than a mutter, but it was used again from time to time and in a 2001 episode she spelled it out, dignifying it as a word and not just a sound.

HOMER: Kids, how would you like to go to Blockoland?
BART AND LISA: Meh.
HOMER: But the TV gave the impression that. . . .
BART: We said meh.
LISA: M-E-H. Meh.

With that example, it has become the Millennial expression of indifference. Urbandictionary.com chose it as Word of the Day for May 22, 2007.

Some tweets from 2012 give the flavor of meh:

> *My sweater has been on backwards all day. Didn't real-*
> *ize it until now. Too lazy to fix it. Today is that kind of*
> *day. #meh*

> *i love getting sick and being completely exhausted during finals week. what i want is lots of sleep, what i need is lots of studying. #meh*

FRIEND (VERB)

How do you make friends? It used to be complicated. You'd usually have to meet a potential friend face to face, take time talking about mutual interests, work or play or live together. If you're awkward, as Millennials often felt, making friends was even harder. That is, till Facebook came along in the first decade of the 21st century. It took the guesswork out of becoming a friend: Just send a friend invitation to someone, and if that person accepts, you're now officially friends. Thanks to Facebook, *friend* became a verb, as in "I friended her last night." You could end a friendship too, by *unfriending* someone, but that was done so quietly that your partner in friendship wouldn't be notified of your action. Only the absence of posts from that friend would tell someone they had been unfriended.

FRIENDS WITH BENEFITS

And that leads to a kind of friendship particularly favored by Millennials: *friends with benefits*.

In contrast with Generation X, being a member of the more privileged Millennials seemed to convey the expectation of an abundance of benefits, ranging from doting parents to doting friends eager for each other's selfies, along with rapid improvements in technology making communication ever more instant and easy. Oh yes, and *friends with benefits* too.

The phrase brings to mind routine fringe benefits, like health insurance and vacation time. It also connects with the routine practice of *friending* people on Facebook. And that's exactly what it's supposed to do, to make something routine out of what had been highly emotional and intimate and often awkward. *Friends with benefits* just adds another to the list of benefits available to Millennials: sex.

It refers to sexual relationships without romantic feelings or commitment, a way for friends to help each other release tensions and enjoy the physical sensations of sex without emotional baggage. Friends who are getting these benefits might have other more serious relationships with boyfriends and girlfriends, but the friends-with-benefits relationship has the presumed benefit of avoiding the complications of those more conventional relationships.

The term *friends with benefits* was picked up from Generation X, which had begun using it in the 1990s. But the term and its abbreviation *fwb* began to be much more widely used around 2000, when the Millennials took to it.

In the 2000s it was well enough established that it inspired how-to books to help Millennials and other friends-with-benefits get through their awkward moments. For it appears that fwb was a little more complex and difficult than it might seem at first. Two "30-something" members of Generation X published *The Happy Hook-up* in 2004: "Mindless fling, harmless hook-up, booty call, friends with benefits. Call it what you want, but let's be honest: more females than ever are choosing to stay single—and sleeping around has become an accepted, if not expected, part of the singles scene. But while casual sex is no longer a girl's dirty little secret, it's not always as easy as it's often made out to be." In that same year the Department of Communication at Michigan State issued a book, *Have Your Cake and Eat it Too: Negotiating a Friends with Benefits Relationship*.

SEXTING

It wasn't as if the Millennials invented sex, but the new technology inspired new ways to hook up. More close-up and immediate, and yet more distant too, both joining and separating by electrons. Less chance for being awkward, therefore. Thanks to technology, sex no longer had to be in person, face to face, body to body. Instead, it could be close up in text and especially pictures, thanks to smartphones and tablets.

Sexting was one of the uses of text messaging, or texting, that became widespread as phones became smarter in the early 2000s. But it gained intensity when selfies were added to the mix.

BOOTY CALL

Sexting and friends with benefits sometimes led to the *booty call*, a phone call late at night asking to meet with the other person for sex. Some booty calls are inspired by the Millennial ailment FOMO, the caller looking for adventure after a disappointing evening. The Financial Samurai website comments, "Some common traits of FOMO sufferers include . . . putting their notifications on vibrate so they can be alert for a 2am booty call."

TRAMP STAMP

Millennials like tattoos. Maybe it's because they like to wear their loves, hates, and hobbies on their skin rather than bothering with sleeves. Or maybe they think of their bodies as blank billboards for advertisements or artwork. They tend to put tattoos in places where ordinary clothes will conceal them, revealing their true selves only in intimate situations and covering up to avoid an employer's displeasure. The *tramp stamp* on a woman's lower back, with a message or design to be revealed only in private, is but one example of the possibilities of self-expression through tattoos.

; (SEMICOLON)

As tattoos, not just pictures and words but punctuation marks can convey messages. Recently the semicolon has been appropriated as a suicide preventive, of all things. "The semicolon is used when a sentence could have ended, but didn't," the Semicolon Movement explains on Tumblr.

> *The movement is for anyone who has ever self-harmed, has a personality disorder, or has tried to commit suicide. The semicolon is a sign of hope. Your sentence is not over yet....*
>
> *If you have ever harmed yourself, attempted suicide, or just want to support the cause, put a semicolon on your wrist or wherever you feel would mean the most. Every time you see it, think of something that makes life worth living.*

The Semicolon Project called for action on a special day: "On April 16, 2014, everyone who self-harms, is suicidal, depressed, has anxiety, is unhappy, going through a broken heart, just lost a loved one, etc. draw a semicolon on your wrist. A semicolon represents a sentence the author could've ended, but chose not to. The author is you and the sentence is your life."

FLASH MOB

The new technology of texting allowed Millennials to invent a new kind of public performance, the *flash mob*. Seemingly out of nowhere, people would step forward out of the crowd at a festival, a wedding, a food court, a museum, a student union, a park, or even Times Square and then perform a previously rehearsed musical piece, dance, pantomime, or a combination of all of them.

Sources agree that the flash mob was invented and named in 2003 by Bill Wasik, an editor at *Harper's*, who staged the first successful flash mob in the rug department of Macy's in Manhattan. Wasik was a Boomer, but from the start the Millennials provided most of the participants, and they have continued ever since, for protests (by Walmart associates in a Raleigh, N.C., store, for example), or more often for celebrations like wedding proposals.

"Hillbillybuddha1," a frequent commentator on YouTube, said "flash mobs are the best thing to come out of the 'hipster generation' but it is leaps and bounds better than anything that came outta my own 'gen x.'" And Cat Flynn, another Millennial, reports, "Flash mobs are still a thing! I actually took part in one in Paris as part of International Pillow Fight Day (yes, really) where I took part in a huge, spontaneous pillow fight outside Gare Saint-Lazare."

OCCUPY

Flash mobs are for fun for a moment. More seriously, in 2011 Millennials gathered outdoors for their style of serious protest. That year they were at the forefront in giving *occupy* a new meaning. It was in the context of *Occupy Wall Street*, sit-ins that began in a little park near Wall Street in New York City and soon spread across the country.

Unlike their Boomer predecessors, who focused on single issues, civil rights, and the Vietnam War in particular, the Millennials who occupied parks and other public spaces across the country in 2011 had many causes. But they all could be boiled down to being in the "99 percent" who didn't have wealth as opposed to the "1 percent" who did.

At the peak of the Occupy movement in October 2011, according to one count there had been Occupy protests in more than six hundred American cities, and quite a few worldwide. Winter brought an end to most of the protests, and they were only sporadically renewed after that. Occupy wasn't going to be a permanent addition to the Millennial vocabulary.

Was Occupy the way the Millennials would save the world, as Strauss and Howe long ago predicted? Evidently not. But perhaps it was a rehearsal for a later time when the issues would be more clear and more urgent. The crisis, according to Strauss and Howe's 1990 crystal ball, would begin in 2005, but it wouldn't reach its climax until 2020 and attain its resolution in 2026. The Millennials still have a decade to show us the way.

HOMELAND GENERATION

(born 2005–)

HOMELAND

Nowadays as each new generation comes along, pundits are ready with labels and dates. Ready or not, here come the Homelanders, supposedly destined to follow the pattern of the Silent Generation as quiet successors to the heroic Millennials.

These post-Millennials, born 2005 and later, are the first generation to grow up post-9/11. Although half of them are yet to be born, in 2015 the oldest are ten years old, not far from beginning to make their linguistic mark in their teen years.

What to call them while they are still in their childhood? In 2006, psychologist Jean Twenge suggested the designation "iGen," reflecting the iProducts of Apple Computer, then already including the iPod and iMac.

Another obvious possibility is "Generation Z," logically following Generations X and Y. But that had the obvious disadvantage of saying nothing about the character of the first 21st-century generation. Safe but unimpressive.

Then came September 11, 2001, a date and event that would overshadow the early lives of the generation. It made "Homeland Generation" a clear choice for the name, "Homelanders" for short. When Howe's company held a naming contest on its website in 2005, Homeland was the overwhelming favorite. Howe himself told *USA Today* in 2012 he wasn't so sure: "We've resisted the temptation to name the next generation until we think the Millennial Generation has run its course." That was prudent. The Silent Generation, for example, didn't get that name until its oldest members were in their mid-twenties and showing their indifference to world affairs.

Nevertheless, the choice of "Homeland Generation" is apt because this will be the first generation to grow up with the post-9/11 meaning of "homeland." Before then, when that word was used at all in American English, it often referred to places of origin of immigrants, not to the United States itself. For example, the 1939 Federal Writers' Project guide to North Carolina tells of the Uharie River: "Local residents spell the name Uwharrie. The valleys were settled by German colonists who may have named it New Werra after a river in their old homeland."

Wikipedia includes cultural connotations of pre-9/11 "homeland" in its definition: "A homeland is the concept of the place to which an ethnic group holds a long history and a deep cultural association."

Indeed, although the word dates from the 17th century in English, Americans pre-9/11 didn't use "homeland" much at all. It wasn't until the Bush administration established the Department of Homeland Security in 2002 that "homeland" became a word in frequent use associated with concerns about terrorism. Its use has spread from the name of that government department to others like Homeland Security majors at colleges and universities.

Its acceptability nowadays is reflected in the choice of "Homeland" as the name of a successful television series on Showtime, premiering in 2011.

Other notable words have come into being in the few years since 2005, especially words associated with new technology like *unfriend, smartphone*, and *tweet*. But those belong to the Millennials. For words other than *Homeland*, we will have to wait until this new generation reaches the teens and begins to develop its own.

What their attitudes and behavior will be like remain to be seen. Predicting in 1997, well before any had been born, Strauss and Howe called them the "New Silent," with "artist" and "adaptive" characteristics like those of the Silents four generations back.

"This generation will have no memory of anything before the financial meltdown of 2008 and the events that are about to unfold in America," Howe said in a 2010 interview for the Casey Report. "If our research is correct, this generation's childhood will be a time of urgency and rapid historical change. Unlike the Millennials, who will remember childhood during the good

times of 1980s and '90s, the Homelanders will recall their childhood as a time of national crisis."

WAIT

But wait. Here's an inkling of how the language of the
Homelanders may develop.

Goran Metcalf, in 2014 an eight-year-old resident of the
Chicago suburb Oak Park, at that age would usually say *wait*
before asking a question:

"Wait.... What's for dinner?"
"Wait.... Where are we going?"
"Wait.... When is my birthday party?"

He even would use it in front of statements:

"Wait.... I want to watch TV."
"Wait.... I'm going over to the neighbor's house."

His father notes that he says it in front of everything. "I'm not
sure if that's something just he does, or if that's how he talks with
his friends. I'm guessing it's not just him."

And there's an obvious reason why he does it, his father says.
It makes you pause and listen to what he has to say. In fact, a year
later his parents were beginning to pick it up too:

Wait.... Adults talking like kids?
Wait.... I sound just like Goran!

This is reminiscent of the Silent Generation's thoughtful approach to the world. All around the country other members of the Homeland Generation are beginning to develop distinctive speech habits like this. What exactly will they decide as their way of expressing themselves? We'll have to wait.